Children of the Covenant

What Christians Should Know About Jews

Dear heavenly Father, I asked The Lord to [illegible] you always in whatever you Do. From Paula.

Thank you for the [illegible] God bless Lynn

to Shine His light upon at Christmas and through the New Year Rosa

Merry Xmas

Thank you for sharing your beautiful gift, knowledge & testimony with us. We love you! Love Denise

Dominique

Thank you + Merry Christmas

Brother [illegible]

Sister Hackney

All the best Brother

Gratitude & Blessings to You! Jackie O'Toole

John [illegible]

Thank you for all your teaching. Louise King

Thanks for your dedicated Teaching Dolores

Best Wishes

Merci Beaucoup pour ce que vous m'apportez spirituellement. Merci de votre exemple. Love Sandrine

Thanks Perry for sharing your insights knowledge of the gospel! Dennis

Children of the Covenant

What Christians Should Know About Jews

Marshall D. Isaacson

First Printing: August 1998

International Standard Book Number:
0-88290-627-5

Library of Congress Catalog Card Number
98-072578

Horizon Publishers' Catalog and Order Number:
1213

Printed and distributed
in the United States of America by

Horizon Publishers
& Distributors, Incorporated

Mailing Address:
P.O. Box 490
Bountiful, Utah 84011-0490

Street Address:
50 South 500 West
Bountiful, Utah 84010

Local Phone: (801) 295-9451
WATS (toll free): 1 (800) 453-0812
FAX: (801) 295-0196

Internet: www.horizonpublishers.com

Contents

Introduction **11**

I Have Graven Thee
Upon the Palms of My Hands 11

Christianity Has Jewish Roots 12

Christ Was Sent to the House of Israel 13

Salvation Is Of the Jews 13

1. The Jew: Both an Enigma and an Anomaly 15

A Culture Preserved for 2000 Years 15

Significant Accomplishments
and Unique Contributions 16

Are Jews Smarter Than Non-Jews? 17

2. How Does One Define a "Jew?" 19

The 1950 Knesset "Law of Return" 20

The Halakhic Definition 20

A Particular Nationality? 21

A Particular Race? 21

A Particular Religion? 22

A Cultural Definition? 23

A Descendency Definition? 23

Identification With the Total Jewish Experience . 24

There Is No Universally Accepted Definition . . . 24

3. A Diminished Spiritual Vitality? 27

Where Is the World's Jewish Population Today? . 27

A Diminished Vitality? 28

Why Did All These People Flock Together? . . . 29
A Disturbing Poll. 30
The Plight of Twentieth-Century Judaism 31
There Can Be No Religion
Without Faith and Feeling 32
The Category of Spiritual Experience Is Absent . 34
A Fertile Field for Preaching the Gospel of Christ 35

4. The Divisions of Judaism 37

Orthodox Judaism. 37
Reform Judaism 39
Conservative Judaism 41
Reconstructionism. 42

5. Christianity and Anti-Semitism 45

Jewish Lack of Differentiation
Between Gentiles and Christians 45
Early Christian Fathers
Blame the Jews for Christ's Crucifixion. . . . 47
Medieval Christian Charges Against the Jews . . 48
The Doctrine of Servitus Judaeorum 49
A Comparison:
Adolf Hitler and John Chrysostom 49
Martin Luther's Anti-Semitism. 51
Jews Slain by the Crusaders 52
The Decisions of Christian Councils. 52
Spain's Edict of Expulsion. 53
The Spanish Inquisition Persecuted the Jews . . 53
Deuteronomy 28 Promised Persecution 54

**6. Why Jews Don't Accept Jesus
as the Son of God. 55**

The Jewish Shema. 55

The Term Elohim 57
Other Evidence Which Shows the Plurality of God 59

7. Why Jews Rejected Jesus as Their Messiah 61

Jesus Failed to Fulfill Jewish Messianic Expectations 61
The Scriptural Standard for Measuring a Prophet's Authenticity 63
Messianic Expectations to Be Fulfilled in a Second Advent 64
Why Many First-Century Jews Were Converted to Jesus 65
Many Jews Today Still Look for the Messiah's Coming 66

8. A Jewish Paradox 67

The Inspiration and Permanence of the Law of Moses 68
The Doctrine of Resurrection 70
The Coming of the Messiah 71
Reflections on Traditions and Dogma 73

9. Jewish Attitudes Toward Sin 75

"Original Sin" Not a Jewish Belief 75
"Original Sin" a Late-Adopted Christian Doctrine 76
Can One "Think" a Sin? 76
Is It the Body or the Soul that Sins? 77
The *Yetzer Ha-ra:* Inclination to Sin 78
Differing Beliefs on the Nature of Repentance . . 79

10. Two Dates That Changed Judaism Forever 85

The Babylonian Captivity

The Oral Law Committed to Writing 85
The Founding of Synagogue Worship 87
Scribes Become Spiritual Leaders 87
The Mishnah Gains Eminence with the Rise of the Rabbis 88
The Talmud 88
A Contrast: Jewish Legalism and Christian Creedism . . . 89

The Destruction of the Second Temple

Moral Deeds Substituted for Altar Sacrifices . . 90
Officiating Priests Replaced by Pious, Ordinary Men 92

11. Bias in Jewish Bible Translations 95

Examples of Unintentional Translation Errors. . 96
Examples of Errors Based on Traditional Biases. 96
Genesis 1:2 97
Isaiah 9:6 98
Isaiah 53:5-8 100
Isaiah 7:14 101
Doctrinal Biases Should Be Set Aside in Scriptural Translations 103

12. Putting Words in Jesus' Mouth 105

A Siege Mentality: Keeping Jews from Examining Jesus' Messianic Claims 105
What Did Jesus Mean? 107

Scripture Twisting—
Portraying Passages Incorrectly
through Altered Meanings 109
A Poignant Reply 113
A Plea for Literacy,
Historical and Doctrinal Honesty 114

13. Like Lambs to the Slaughter 115

Where Was Their Will to Live? 115
Jewish Uprising Against Their Tormentors . . . 116
Passive Acceptance of Gentile Pogroms. 116
Four Attitudes Concerning Jewish Deaths . . . 118
Negative Observations on the Nature of Man. . 121
Positive Observations on the Nature of Man . . 121

Conclusion 123

The Need for Internalized Worship 123
Pray That the Jews
May Recognize Their Messiah 124

Endnotes 127

Index 135

About the Author 143

Dedication

In memory of my parents,
Hyman and Gertrude Isaacson,
who left this world
without ever having known
the fulfillment
of their own Judaism—the Messiah.

Introduction

I Have Graven Thee Upon the Palms of My Hands

There is a widely-held belief among Christians today that God has forgotten the Jews and has withdrawn His blessing from them as a special people. Yes, it is true (and also scriptural) that God no longer makes a distinction between Jew and Gentile where salvation is concerned. Today, people of all nations are offered forgiveness equally through the atoning death of Jesus Christ. However, as far as the time of Jews' special relationship with God is concerned, it went on hold almost 2000 years ago. It will not begin again until Jesus Himself starts it up in preparation for His millennial reign here on earth.

Has God really forgotten His ancient people? Not according to scripture He hasn't. Listen to what the Lord says through the prophet Isaiah:

> But Zion said, The Lord hath forsaken me, and my LORD hath forgotten me.
>
> Can a woman forget her nursing child, that she should not have compassion on the son of her womb? yea, they may forget, yet will I not forget thee.

> Behold, I have graven thee upon the palms of my hands; thy walls are continually before me (Isaiah 49: 14-16).

The eleventh chapter of Romans begins with the reassuring words of the apostle Paul, "I say then, Hath God cast away his people? God forbid." In fact, the entire eleventh chapter is a testimonial to the proposition that though the Jew has temporarily lost his unique relationship with God, the time is coming when once again Israel shall be lifted to a position of prominence among the nations and shall once more become the "apple of God's eye."

However, the purpose of this study is not to aggrandize Jews but to glorify Jesus. It also is written to inspire as well as to inform, to strengthen Christians' faith through helping them understand the people and religion that laid the foundation of their faith. Keep in mind that without the Jews there would be no Jesus, and without the Bible there would be no Jews. Indeed, there is every good reason to say that Jews are appropriately called the "people of the Book."

Furthermore, not only do the Jews come on the biblical scene in the early chapters of Genesis to do God's bidding, but representatives of the House of Israel are also the last group on earth to do God's bidding prior to the millennium—the 144,000 of the Book of Revelation.

Christianity Has Jewish Roots

Considering that the Lord was a Jew; that all of the writers of the Bible were Jews (with the exception of Luke); that the written Word of God in the Old Testament was painstakingly copied and transmitted to us over thousands of years by Jews; and that the early Church was comprised primarily of Jews; it is surprising how little interest modern Christians have regarding God's ancient people. This is true, despite the fact that more often than not, most Sunday sermons make reference to Jews in one way or another. We Christians certainly know about doctrines, dogmas and duties, but we know precious little concerning those from whose midst came our Lord and Savior.

Remember, at the beginning of His ministry, Jesus was concerned only for His Jewish people. To His disciples He instructed,

> . . . Go not into the way of the gentiles, and into any city of the Samaritans enter not:
>
> But go rather to the lost sheep of the house of Israel (Matthew 10:5-6).

Christ Was Sent to the House of Israel

Of Himself, Jesus declared, ". . . I am not sent but unto the lost sheep of the house of Israel" (Matthew 15:24). Yet, because of 2000 years of Jewish refusal to embrace the truth that *Y'shua ha-Mashiah*, (Joshua the Messiah, Jesus the Christ) came to earth to offer Himself as the Jews' sacrificial Passover Lamb, the non-Jewish world has become the primary beneficiary of God's gift of His Son to mankind.

Salvation Is Of the Jews

It was Jesus Himself who told the Samaritan woman at the well that "Salvation is of the Jews"

(John 4:22). Almost everything we Christians hold spiritually dear has come to us through the Jews.

Perhaps it is time that we inform ourselves concerning the only people over whom Christ Jesus ever lamented heartbreakingly when He said:

> O Jerusalem, Jerusalem, thou that killest the prophets, and stonest them who are sent unto thee; how often would I have gathered thy children together even as a hen gathereth her chickens under her wings, and ye would not!
>
> Behold, your house is left unto you desolate.
>
> For I say unto you, Ye shall not see me henceforth, till ye shall say, Blessed is he that cometh in the name of the Lord (Matthew 23:37-39).

But until that day when all Jews shall physically see their glorified Messiah, the only glimpse of Him they probably will ever have is the Jesus they see in you and in me. Therefore, the more you and I know about the Jews—about what they do and what they believe—the more easily will they be able to see Jesus in both our words and in our daily actions. To such an end, this study is dedicated.

1

The Jew: Both an Enigma and an Anomaly

A Culture Preserved for 2000 Years

As a point of departure for this study, it might be well to consider the societal uniqueness of Jews. For example, most cultural anthropologists agree that never in human history has a distinctive people been driven out of their land, scattered across the face of the earth, forced to integrate with foreign cultures, and then almost 2000 years later, not only have they returned to their ancestral homeland, but they also returned with their language, culture, and religion intact. Such is the history of the Jewish people—a history that defies all rational explanation, and marks the Jews as a unique anthropological enigma. Certainly this cannot be attributed to the good intentions of Gentiles, for historically they have done everything within their power to eradicate the Jews. However, these ancient people have survived many of the very cultures that sought to destroy them.

Significant Accomplishments and Unique Contributions

In addition to being an enigma, Jews also represent an anomaly in our society. Consider the following statistics as evidence of that anomaly:

1. World Jewish population is less than 1/2 of 1% of the total, yet of the 375 Nobel Prizes awarded between 1901 and 1968, Jews won 22% of them.

2. Between 1901 and 1965, 67 American scientists won Nobel Prizes. Of these, eighteen (27%) were awarded to Jews (Jews at the time comprising only 3% of the U.S. population). This is nine times the number of Nobel Laureates that might be statistically expected.[1]

3. A further anomaly regarding Jews is seen in the fact that they are over-represented in the professions by 231% in medicine; 308% in medical specialties; 478% in psychiatry; 299% in dentistry; 265% in law; and 283% in mathematics.[2]

4. Also, as a proportion of the U.S. population, Jewish students are over-represented by 260% in colleges and by 365% in the most prestigious institutions.[3]

5. Beyond this, Jews have contributed significantly to man's physical well-being. For example: (1) Dr. Minofsky discovered insulin; (2) Casimir Funk discovered vitamins; (3) Jonas Salk discovered a vaccine against polio; (4) Paul Ehrlich fathered the science of immunology; (5) Selman

Waksman developed antibiotics; (6) Tadeus Reichstein discovered cortisone; (7) Karl Landsteiner discovered blood groupings.

6. Finally, three men who profoundly influenced the twentieth century were all Jews: (1) Karl Marx did so politically; (2) Sigmund Freud intellectually; and (3) Albert Einstein scientifically. Suffice to say that the statistically insignificant Jew has impacted our world and our lives beyond all logical and reasonable expectations.

Are Jews Smarter Than Non-Jews?

Any discussion of Jewish intellectual accomplishments must raise an obvious question: Are Jews really smarter than non-Jews? For example, if some of what we are intellectually is genetically inherited, then are Western Jewish children born smarter than Western non-Jewish children? Dr. Ernest van den Haag, professor of social philosophy at New York University, thought so, and suggested the following hypothesis to explain why.

During the Middle Ages, and for hundreds of years before and after, the only career that offered advancement and intellectual challenge to talented sons born to non-Jewish parents of both high and low station was that of becoming a cleric and serving the Church. However, such a life-choice came at a considerable price—that of celibacy. This resulted in society's mounting loss of a vital gene pool emanating from these most gifted and intelligent young Gentile men. Thus, for hundreds of years those bright genes simply disappeared—

never having been passed on to successive generations.[4]

Conversely, for intellectually ambitious young Jewish men of that period the situation was just the reverse. They became rabbis, were encouraged to marry young, often won the hands of daughters from wealthy families, and generally had more children than did non-scholastic Jewish men. The result was that for a thousand years each succeeding generation born to these rabbis had an ever-increasing pool of bright genes upon which to draw.

Are Jews smarter than non-Jews? No one can really say, but one thing is clear: Jews have continually excelled intellectually beyond the norms of all societal and numerical expectations. Since there appears to be no earthly answer to this anomaly, perhaps, then, there is a heavenly one.

2

How Does One Define a "Jew?"

Some years ago I debated with an orthodox rabbi through "Letters to the Editor." He argued that if a Jew converted to Christianity he was no longer a Jew. The issue obviously was unresolved, but in my own mind, the question of just who or what is a Jew really needed to be settled. For example, one sometimes hears people say that the Jews are responsible for this or for that situation. Unfortunately, it is not at all clear who is being accused here. Are they (1) those living in Israel, (2) those who practice the Jewish faith, or (3) those who were born of Jewish parents? These different groups are not all necessarily the same.

Viewed another way, it is quite logical to say that all Chinese are Orientals, but all Orientals are not Chinese. However, the same reasoning cannot be applied to Jews because there is no generally agreed-upon category into which "Jew" fits. Are all Jews members of a particular race or adherents to a specific form of worship, or are they citizens of a particular country? Exactly who or what a Jew is remains today as one of the least agreed upon of all issues—even among Jews themselves.

The 1950 Knesset "Law of Return"

A definition was required of the Israeli Knesset (parliament) following Israel's having been declared a sovereign state in May of 1948. Specifically, who is a Jew and entitled therefore, to come to Israel? In 1950, the Knesset enacted the "Law of Return," which was secular legislation to guarantee that ". . . every Jew has a right to come to this country as an *oleh*" (a Jew immigrating to Israel for settlement). However, the law merely stated what a Jew may do, not what a Jew is.

The Halakhic Definition

For centuries prior to the Law of Return, the *halakhic* definition of a Jew was anyone born of a Jewish mother. (*Halakah* is "the walk" in life; the day-by-day guidelines of law, ordinance, and practical rule designating the Jewish way of life.) Authority for this definition came from the *Talmud* (the Jews' "Oral" law reduced to written form):

> Thy son by an Israelite woman is called thy son, but thy son by a heathen [Gentile] woman is not called thy son.

Any child, therefore, born of a non-Jewish mother of a mixed marriage, had to undergo ritual conversion to be a Jew, even though his/her father was a Jew. However, the problem here is that the term "Israelite woman" is not defined. Is she a woman born of a Jewish mother, or could she be a Gentile convert qualifying as an "Israelite woman," or is she simply a woman, Jewish-born or not, who lives among the Jews? It is not at all clear, and so the question remains unanswered. "What does it mean to be Jewish?"

Today in Israel the question of who is a Jew (not who is an Israeli citizen) is still argued. For example, is a Gentile who undergoes conversion through a "Reform" (liberal) synagogue viewed as a *halakhic* Jew according to orthodox believers? What about the born and bred Jew who no longer practices Judaism as a religion. Is he still to be considered a Jew? It's really not at all clear.

A Particular Nationality?

So who then is a Jew? Is it someone who is of a particular nationality? No, for there are Jews who live in almost every nation on earth: England, Russia, France, Brazil, New Zealand, Japan, Mexico. You name it and there are Jews who were born and raised there, and are nationals of that particular country.

A Particular Race?

Then is a Jew someone who belongs to a particular race? (This happens to be the most widely-accepted non-Jewish concept of a Jew.) No, because there are Caucasian Jews, Black Jews (thousands of them called "Falasha" who in 1991 were rescued from Ethiopia by the Israelis). There are Indian Jews, Hispanic Jews, Japanese Jews, and even a sizable colony of Chinese Jews in K'ai-feng Fu in central China. These last are not

European Jewish merchants doing business in China, but are instead, genuine ethnic Chinese.

Beyond this, if we argue "race" (blood) as that which defines a Jew (as did the Nazi Nuremberg Laws of 1937), then blood becomes the sole criterion. Any Gentile wanting to convert to Judaism would of necessity have to undergo a complete transfusion—an absolutely absurd requirement. To put it another way, if "race" defines a Jew, then a prospective convert would have no more chance of becoming a Jew than would Albert Einstein of becoming a Negro or an Oriental.

A Particular Religion?

Since neither nationality nor race seem able to clearly define a Jew, what about religion? Is someone who observes and practices the Hebrew faith a Jew? Perhaps so. At least this definition is closely related to the connotation of the word "Jew."

Consider the following example for a moment. If I point to an American and say that he is an Italian, or an Ethiopian, or a Swede, or a Mexican, or a Samoan, absolutely nothing of a religious nature comes to mind. But if I point to an American and say that he is a Jew, you immediately become at least vaguely aware of his being identified in some ancient, mystical way with the worship of Jehovah God.

Such is the connotative power of the word "Jew," and therefore perhaps this universally recognized connotation is the most convincing determiner of just who is a Jew. However, to append the requirement that such religious faith must be Orthodox as opposed to "Reform" or "Conservative," is to argue content—not substance—and therefore contributes nothing to the definition.

A Cultural Definition?

Given the foregoing, have we finally arrived at an acceptable understanding of who is a Jew? No, not really, because what do we do with those tens of thousands of born and bred Jews who no longer practice Judaism as a religion or who have rejected God altogether (particularly those embittered by the Holocaust), but still staunchly maintain their identity as Jews? In this case, we might be better off to seek a "cultural" definition—one which not only transcends nationality and race, but religion as well, and focuses instead on *Bet Yisrael* (the House of Israel).

A Descendency Definition?

An even closer cultural identity with Judaism is found throughout the Pentateuch (the first five books of the Old Testament) in the phrase *B'nai Yisrael* (the children of Israel). Thus, based upon the negative principle of "guilt by association," a more universal definition of "Jew" would be one who simply acknowledges identity with the ancient Hebrew family chosen by God in the Bible. This, in itself, would make one a Jew regardless of whether one was born into Judaism, married into it, converted to it, or, in this case, simply possessed a personal sense of belonging to, and identifying with, the 3500-year legacy of the Jewish people. Such a definition knows no limitations; not nationality, nor race, nor religion.

Identification With the Total Jewish Experience

Certainly I, as a Hebrew Christian, am profoundly aware of my Jewishness—not only because my parents and grandparents were Jews, and because I was raised in a religious Jewish home, but also because I have a deep abiding sense of identification with the total experience of the Jewish people. This, as much as race, nationality or religion, is perhaps what really makes one a Jew. Admittedly, however, this definition is not cast in bronze and is surely not universally accepted.

There Is No Universally Accepted Definition

Hence, we end up where we began. We have a question rather than an answer. Frankly, only individual and group definitions of "Jew" exist. Certainly nothing approaching a universally accepted definition can be found, not even among Jews themselves. But here is a word of encouragement to my Hebrew-Christian brothers and sisters, who have had their Jewishness challenged by other Jews. In his book, *Who Was A Jew*, Lawrence H. Scheffman tells us to take heart and ignore the barbs of our uninformed brethren after the flesh:

> . . . heresy, no matter how great, was never seen as cutting the heretic's tie to Judaism. Not even outright apostasy could overpower the *halakhic* criteria for Jewish identification . . . When the method of excommunication was used to separate heretics from the Jewish community in the Middle Ages, even this measure, which was to a great extent a medieval *halakhic* development, did not in any way cancel the Jewish status of the excommunicant. Indeed, regardless of

the transgressions of a Jew, he was a Jew under any and all circumstances, even though his rights within *halakhah* might be limited as a result of his actions.[1]

What is the centuries-old hope and longing of the Jewish people? It is the long-awaited coming of the Messiah. Therefore, if a Jew embraces Jesus Christ as the Messiah, does he suddenly cease being a Jew simply because he claims to have found the Messiah? At worst, all that the Jewish community can say to a Hebrew Christian, is that they vigorously disagree with his choice of Jesus as the Messiah. But it is ridiculous for them to say that because a Jew has found the Messiah, he is no longer a Jew. Yet that is the present custom among the vast majority of Jews today when one of their number realizes that Jesus of Nazareth was and is the Messiah. How is that justified?

As the Jews themselves often say when confronted with a situation that defies conventional wisdom, "Go figure."

3

A Diminished Spiritual Vitality?

Where Is the World's Jewish Population Today?

It is interesting to look at statistics which shape Judaism today. Figures published in the *USA Today* on May 4, 1998 indicated that about 95 percent of the world's Jewish population of nearly 14 million people live in one of ten countries:

1.	United States of America	5,900,000
2.	Israel	4,800,000
3.	France	600,000
4.	Russia	550,000
5.	Ukraine	400,000
6.	Canada	360,000
7.	United Kingdom	300,000
8.	Argentina	250,000
9.	Brazil	130,000
10.	South Africa	106,000

Obviously, a population this large and widespread has a variety of national and cultural influences which influence its attitudes and life orientation. With that in mind, the observations in this chapter must be perceived as an attempt to speak in a broad generality, recognizing that there inevitably must be many exceptions to the overall picture painted here.

A Diminished Vitality?

The best place to begin this study of what Christians don't know about Jews is to realize that the vitality of Judaism, which sustained it through thousands of years of persecutions, invasions and banishments, may no longer exist for some Jews today.

Certainly there are many synagogues today, but according to a host of observers within the Jewish community itself, they are primarily religious centers in which only a listless form of tradition and ritual are practiced.

In the opinion of various commentators, the pursuit of religious truth, unfortunately, is of little concern in many of these places of worship. Neither is spiritual nor even intellectual stimulation to be found there. Jewish author, Max Brod, made this observation as early as 1934:

> I am constantly amazed at the naïveté of our teachers and leaders who are surprised when I tell them that the best of our youth, our intellectuals, become Christians out of conviction. . . . Our leaders do not believe it. To them a Jew never becomes a Christian unless he wants to better his position. That Christianity has drawn to itself such noble [Jewish] souls as Pascal, Novalis, Kirkegaard, Amiel, Claudel,

> Dostoevski, etc., and that it exercises a most overwhelming influence on the most earnest truth seekers among us, of that our teachers know nothing.[1]

Why Did All These People Flock Together?

Admittedly Brod spoke as a layman, a rabbinical outsider, but this same recognition of the lack of religious vitality of Judaism in general, and of the spiritual malaise of rabbis in particular, was addressed by one of the most revered rabbis in America, Professor Abraham J. Heschel of the Jewish Theological Seminary. At the Fifty-third Annual Convention of Conservative Rabbis held in Atlantic City, Dr. Heschel addressed the over two hundred delegates in the following heart-searching words:

> There are many who can execute and display many fireworks, but who knows how to kindle a spark in the darkness of the soul? . . . Ours is a great responsibility. We demand that people come to the synagogue instead of playing golf or making money or going on a picnic. Why? Don't we mislead them? People take their precious time off to attend services, some even arrive with profound expectations. But what do they get? . . . Sometimes even the rabbi sits in his chair wondering: "Why did all these people flock together?"[2]

Concluding the discussion on how to revitalize prayer in the synagogue, Dr. Heschel continued:

> I spoke in sincerity, in wholeheartedness, out of my deep respect and affection for the members of the Rabbinical assembly; I spoke in the spirit of self-criticism. . . . I have been deeply bothered all my life by my own failure in obtaining *kavanak* [spiritual concentrations] when I pray myself. I have a great many

> difficulties and doubts and do not oversimplify the religious situation. But let us stop avoiding the issue by overrating the periphery: prayer is not the main issue. The issue of prayer is God. And the problem is not synagogue attendance—it is spiritual attendance. It is not how to fill the buildings, how to attract bodies to enter a space of a temple, but how to inspire souls to enter an hour of spiritual concentration in the presence of God.[3]

A Disturbing Poll

This exposure to a troubled rabbinic soul should come as no surprise when one looks at the overall spiritual concerns of American rabbis. *In Disciples of the Wise*, Joseph Zeitlin cites the results of a religious poll taken among American rabbis. The results demonstrate the spiritual poverty of many of these religious leaders.

On being asked for a definition of God, most rabbis advocated that "God is the sum total of forces which make for our greater intelligence, beauty, and goodness."[4] On being asked about the Bible, more than two-thirds of the Rabbinate did not accept the view attributing the authorship of the Pentateuch to Moses.

Further, more than half of those who replied to the questionnaire rejected the literal interpretation of the biblical account of The Creation.

Regarding prayer, the majority of the Rabbinate did not believe that the function of prayer is to bring Divine aid to the suppliant.

Also, on the question of sin, only a minority of those who answered conceived of sin as originating in the base impulses of human nature. On the other hand, the great majority believed that the concept of sin, which needs greater emphasis in our age, is to be expressed in social terms. That is to say: as (1) harm to neighbor, friends, or business associates; (2) harm to society; or (3) support of or acquiescence to accepted institutions which are socially harmful.

On salvation, many of the rabbis believed that it is an achievement of an integrated personality. According to others, it is participation in efforts for social progress.

What we have here is, admittedly, the result of an impersonal, objective survey, one in which the head—not the heart—is revealed.

The Plight of Twentieth-Century Judaism

A more personal observation of what he viewed as the plight of twentieth-century Judaism was made by Rabbi Joel Blau in *The Jewish Spectator* of 1949:

> Great as is the tragedy of the Jew, greater still is the tragedy of Judaism. What greater tragedy than the life of a people that has lost its God. . . . So far as synagogues are concerned, they seem beyond resuscitation. There is little left. Talmudical Judaism has broken down—it seems irrevocably. The old ceremonial law is honored more in the breach than in the observance. What then is left? A lifeless formalism that no one takes seriously; here and there a pathetic bit of folklore in connection with death or marriage

> customs; a little ostentatious charity; all of this scarcely relieved by the annual visit to the synagogue on the Day of Atonement. It is as if the spirit has fled the husk. The old words fail to move, the old ideas fail to thrill. And there is no Sinai from whose thundering top the God of our fathers may speak to His backsliding children.[5]

Has ever a more heartrending observation been made by one who realizes that the very marrow of his spiritual life has somehow drained away?

Christians experience something of what Rabbi Blau felt every time we read those thought-provoking words of Paul in which he says:

> For if the dead rise not, then is not Christ raised:
>
> And if Christ be not raised, your faith is vain; ye are yet in your sins.
>
> Then they also which are fallen asleep in Christ are perished.
>
> If in this life only we have hope in Christ, *we are of all men most miserable* (1 Corinthians 15:16-19, emphasis mine).

If this were the case, then our Sunday morning worship services, our songs of praise, and our earnest prayers would amount to nothing more than a spiritual exercise in futility, a whistling in a religious graveyard.

There Can Be No Religion Without Faith and Feeling

And yet, this, perhaps, is the general condition of Judaism today. Rituals and prayers are performed as a matter of fact—not as a matter of faith.

Listen to the lament of Rabbi Nathan A. Barack in *The Contemporary Jewish Record*, August, 1942:

> We may still speak of ourselves as a religious people. The fact is: we were; we no longer are. Many of us look back nostalgically to our religious days; our longing does not restore them. Obviously one is religious neither by the routine observance of Jewish customs nor by the mere attendance at Friday evening services. There can be no religion without faith and feeling. We lack both elements. Any sincere intelligent layman will readily admit to the fact. To open-eyed rabbis it is a painful reality in the pursuit of their daily duties . . . Today, most Jews are no longer able to pray . . . Our people do not pray because they cannot. One prays to God not by addressing Him verbally. One must know in one's heart to whom he prays. We do not.[6]

Can you imagine what it would be like to pray, yet know that your prayers rise no higher than the ceiling of your room? Are you able to glean just a little of the spiritual malaise that afflicts many Jews, the world over, as they mechanically go through their synagogue worship without ever experiencing the nearness of God?

Imagine yourself in a church in which the speaker gets up on Sunday morning to deliver a sermon and finds himself having to say *something* instead of having something to *say*. Imagine yourself in a church where the leader has no testimony, the choir has no enthusiasm, and the congregation has no joy. Such is the sad condition of much of Judaism today.

Listen to the heartbroken confession of a rabbi that appeared in *The Jewish Spectator* of 1949:

> I feel so very inadequate in the rabbinate at times. I feel I have nothing to give my people. How can I make God real to them? How can I make them believe that God really hears their prayers when I myself am not quite certain. Of course I believe in God, otherwise I could not get up in front of my congregation. But there is uncertainty in my belief. I have no clear conception of God. But how can one place implicit trust in God when one is not utterly certain of Him and His concern for men. I lack certainty in the divine origin of the Law and because of this I am ineffective.[7]

One cannot help but grieve for this man, this rabbinical leader of a congregation of spiritually hungering Jews, who look to him to provide manna for their hungry souls. Yet this rabbi is not alone in his feelings of religious ineptitude. Also wandering in this wilderness of spiritual uncertainty and isolation from God are not simply a handful of other rabbis, but hundreds, perhaps thousands of them.

The Category of Spiritual Experience Is Absent

Certainly Nathan Glazer came to this conclusion in his article on the absence of spiritual experience in Judaism, as quoted in *Commentary*, 1956:

> There is nothing in American Jewish literature—and many rabbis have written their autobiographies—that can find its place in any anthology of religious experience. In the biographies of American Jews and rabbis, one will find passions engaged by the problems of Zionism, by politics, by reform movements, by the conflict of different organizations within Jewish life—but the category of spiritual experience, as ordinarily defined, is absent.[8]

Obviously Judaism is not fully alive and well today, but is instead, in the throes of spiritual malnutrition. The pathetic thing in all of this is that the patient doesn't even know he is sick or, worse yet, doesn't want to be told. But telling him is exactly what Jesus Christ called His followers to do. Taking the Gospel into all the world includes taking it to God's ancient people as well. In fact, the Apostle Paul made it a priority: "For I am not ashamed of the Gospel of Christ: for it is the power of God unto salvation to everyone that believeth; to the Jew first, and also to the Greek" (Romans 1:16).

A Fertile Field for Preaching the Gospel of Christ

In this regard, a particularly fertile field for taking the Gospel to Jews is the former Soviet Union. In an article entitled "Bringing Jews to Jesus in Russia," appearing in an American Jewish magazine, the following facts are stated:

> According to a 1994 survey conducted by the Russian Academy of Sciences and the University of Michigan's director of Judaic studies . . . a third of the people in Russia today whose documents call them Jewish by "nationality" consider themselves to be Jewish by faith. Another 13 percent say they lean toward Christianity. More than half say they feel no religious allegiance at all.[9]
>
> Says Adolf Shayervich, who during the Soviet regime was installed as Russia's chief rabbi and continues in that position today, "Many [Jews] here feel they can remain Jewish by nationality but be Christian by religion."[10]
>
> Ariveh Brotkin, director of the Or Avner Jewish day school in St. Petersburg says:

> Jews are the kind of people who actively search for their spiritual potential . . . Many people are simply not sure where to go. As a result, many Jews have followed their spiritual quest not simply into "Messianic Judaism" but into unadulterated Christianity . . . In some cases, even the exceptional Jew who has some sort of observant background [in Judaism] is attracted by something in the church that had eluded him or her in synagogue.[11]

Surely the Jewish field of missionary work is ripe for harvest, but the workers are far too few. Remember in the eighth chapter of Acts, where the Spirit of God told Philip to join the Ethiopian treasurer in his chariot, where he was trying to understand the words of Isaiah? What did the Ethiopian answer in reply to Philip's question? "Understandest thou what thou readest?" The Ethiopian said, "How can I except some man should guide me?" (Acts 8:31)

Is the Jew any less needy in understanding God's plan of salvation than the Ethiopian? Certainly not, but you and I are going to have to hop up there in the chariot with the Jew, to reveal to him from the Word of God, the Messiahship of the Lord Jesus.

4
The Divisions of Judaism

Many Christians believe that all Jews are solidly united, following one faith, with only one set of tenets. Such was the case before the Middle Ages, but since then, Judaism has fragmented into denominations. Just as Christianity divided into distinct orders, such as Baptist, Methodist, Presbyterian, etc., so Judaism has splintered into four separate denominations. Each has followed a distinct theological path. These four major groups are Orthodox, Reform, Conservative, and Reconstructionism.

Orthodox Judaism

Orthodoxy, as an institution, can be traced back to the eighth century A.D. However, its basic rituals and tenets go all the way back to Moses and to the commandments he received upon Sinai. Orthodoxy is strict, demanding, and fraught with literally hundreds of rules and regulations. One ancient rabbi calculated that there are 613 biblical commandments. Those which are affirmative number 248, supposedly corresponding to the number of bones in the human body. The negative commandments number 365, corresponding to the number of days in the year. For the Jew, failure to keep even one of these injunctions constitutes sin.

Added to the 613 biblical injunctions are innumerable other do's and don'ts, evolved through hundreds of years of rabbinic interpretations of the Scriptures. The sheer number and minutiae of these rabbinic instructions are overwhelming. For example, it is not enough for a Jewish mourner to simply mourn the loss of a loved one; there is a prescribed method of mourning and a period for doing so:

1. the bereaved is to lament and weep for three days,
2. he is restricted to home for seven days,
3. he is to wear somber clothes and abstain from personal adornment for thirty days, and
4. he is to abstain from pleasures and amusements for one year.

Orthodoxy not only dictates how and when a Jew should worship, but also proscribes almost every other aspect of his life—from the moment he arises in the morning until the moment he retires at night. It shapes the adherent's outlook on food, clothes, business, sex, marriage, and even the ritual washing for women following their menstrual periods.

Orthodoxy, in this form, continues to exist even today. In fact, recently it has declared that Jews who practice non-orthodox Judaism are not Jews at all. Such a statement came from the Union of Orthodox Rabbis in the U.S. and Canada, in which they asserted that Conservative and Reform (liberal) Jews are in fact, no longer Jews.

Outrage against this rabbinic action was immediate and swift. In *The Jewish Journal*, there appeared an essay entitled "They Say We Are Not Jews." The writer angrily challenges the authority of these orthodox rabbis to decide who is and who is not a Jew. Even several orthodox rabbis wrote in to denounce such ecclesiastical arrogance. The Union of Orthodox Rabbis stated that the motive for their declaration was the hope that it would "draw Conservative and Reform Jews out of their heretical temples."[1]

Reform Judaism

It took hundreds of years, but eventually there was a breakaway from orthodoxy. Prior to the 1700's, Jews of Western Europe lived in ghettos where the authority of rabbis was absolute with regard to religious, criminal, and civil matters. The ghettos proved quite effective in keeping new ideas out of the community, and in so doing, enabled Jews to live their lives in blind, unquestioned obedience to the Torah (Bible) and to the Talmud (the written Oral Law and its rabbinical commentaries).

However, within the eighteenth century came the Age of Enlightenment and the Age of Reason, together with one other important event—emancipation. When the ghetto walls fell, so did the Jews' unquestioned acceptance of their religious teachings. Suddenly, Jews were part of a larger community than that of the ghetto. As a result, they were forced to reexamine their religious beliefs and practices, and to adjust them to the ways of living and belonging to a much larger, non-Jewish society. Thus it was, that from the rubble of the ghetto walls, a new movement in religious thinking arose—Reform Judaism.

The intellectual seeds of the Reform movement came from Moses Mendelssohn, a German Jew who sought to synthesize Judaism with culture. The movement began early in the nineteenth century in Germany and was solidly rooted in eighteenth–century "Enlightenment." Specifically, it was the belief that behind the different religions there was a common faith—the religion of "humanity." Reformers held that men were basically good and that the world was getting better, and because of this, a new form of Judaism was needed—one that would fit the modern Jew. To them, orthodoxy was just too unenlightened and unappealing, and many emancipated Jews wanted to throw off the restraints of Mosaic legislation and focus instead on mankind.

Rabbi Morris N. Kertzer put his finger on the real pulse of Reform Judaism when he said that what Reform Jews believe about the Bible, about miracles, and about life after death, is secondary to what they believe about human potentialities and about Reform Jews' responsibilities toward their fellow man. Reformers abandoned the requirement that only Hebrew be spoken in the synagogues. They also rejected the ideas that there would be a resurrection of the dead and that there would be a coming of a personal messiah.

Conservative Judaism

However, such a radical departure from orthodoxy was too big a step for many Jews to take. As a result, there arose a third division in Judaism—the Conservative movement. Concerning Reform Judaism's radical departure from orthodoxy, Rabbi Alexander Kohut, professor of Midrash and Talmud at the Jewish Theological Seminary of America, said:

> A reform which seeks to progress without the Mosaic-rabbinical tradition is a [deformity] skeleton without flesh and sinew, without spirit and heart . . .[2]

Conservatism began with Zacharias Frankel, an eminent rabbinical scholar who, in the mid-1850's, felt that he was unable to identify with either the strictures of traditional orthodoxy or with the social and religious liberalism of the Reform movement.

Conservative Judaism has proven to be the middle ground between orthodoxy and reform. For example, *Halakhah* (the "walk" governing all Jewish actions in every-day life) is still binding on all conservatives, but may be adjusted to accommodate changes in one's personal life or in societal circumstances. The use of Hebrew is encouraged in services but is not mandatory. Belief in the resurrection and in the coming of a Messiah are left open to individual interpretation.

The large number of Jews pouring into the United States during the late 1800's from Eastern Europe found conservatism much more palatable than orthodoxy, and as a result, conservatism became the largest religious Jewish movement in America. As Rabbi Isaac Wise once said: "It is possible to live as Jews in the synagogue and as Americans everywhere else."[3]

Reconstructionism

The fourth denomination in Judaism is Reconstructionism, which seeks to secularize the synagogue so that not only is it a place of worship, but more importantly, it is a place where families can gather for non-religious purposes. This idea of a "synagogue center" came from Mordecai Kaplan in 1918. It seeks to cater to the entire social need of the family. Such activities as men and women's clubs, social and athletic groups, sewing and card-playing groups, boy scouts and girl scouts, plus many more activities are offered. Suffice it to say that such an approach to Judaism has met a genuine need in the life of American Jews, and as a result, the movement has continued to grow.

Whether the rabbis like it or not, they have been forced to go along with this new idea since the American synagogue is lay-controlled and, therefore, it's what the laity wants—not what the rabbi wants. Still, there are genuine rabbinic misgivings about any Jewish religious movement that takes such a radical departure from traditional forms of worship. Rabbi David Aronson gave voice to this fear when he said:

> A community that accepts the philosophy that a gymnasium is as essential to Jewish life as a synagogue, and a Jewish basketball team as conducive to Jewish survival as a Talmud Torah [a Jewish school] is on its way to Jewish extinction."[4]

Hopefully, this brief glimpse into the various denominations within Judaism will dispel the all-too-pervasive concept among others that all Jews hold identical religious convictions. Yes, they all believe in God, but that's as far as it goes. There is no personal Savior, whose sacrificial death and glorious resurrection unifies them in the hope of an eternity with God.

5
Christianity and Anti-Semitism

Jewish Lack of Differentiation Between Gentiles and Christians

Of paramount importance in understanding the gulf separating Jews from Christians is the realization that most Jews see no difference between being a Gentile and being a Christian. To the average Jew, the world is comprised of only two major classifications: Jews and Gentiles.

There is no third category called "Christians." For Jews, if you are not born a Jew, then you are born a Christian ("Gentile" being implied and understood).

An example of this classic Jewish perspective is this statement by Dr. Leo Trepp, rabbi, college professor and author of *Eternal Faith, Eternal People*. He writes the following:

> Colleges and universities placed restrictions on the number of Jewish students they would admit. . . . It

> forced the Jewish student, even in high school, to work twice as hard for good grades as his *Christian* fellow (emphasis mine).[1]

Also,

> They [Jews] were excluded from hotels with "restricted clientele," from certain health resorts, country clubs and Greek letter organizations. . . . A curtain of separation still seems to settle between *Christians* and Jews at five o'clock every evening (emphasis mine).[2]

Jews seldom consider the fact that you cannot be *born* a Christian; you must decide to become one by accepting Christ and His gospel, and by being *born again*. Even Nicodemus was confused by this concept, for when Jesus told him that he must be "born again," the old Jew asked, ". . . How can a man be born when he is old? can he enter a second time into his mother's womb, and be born?" (John 3:4).

This Jewish propensity to equate Christians with Gentiles had its origin in Christianity's long involvement with anti-Semitism. (May I pause here to say that as a Hebrew Christian, this was a difficult essay for me to write because as a follower of the Messiah—Jesus—I felt deep shame at Christianity's historic record of anti-Semitism. Compounding this was my anger, as a Jew, at the hundreds of years of inhumanity and persecution heaped upon my people by those who justified their actions in the name of God and the Church.)

The historical fact of Christendom's persecution of the Jews cannot be denied. Yet, because it was done out of vengeance, ignorance and fear, it certainly should be forgiven—though not forgotten, as an important lesson for mankind. Having said this, let us move on to consider why Jewish aversion to Christianity is based as much on church history as it is on theological differences.

In the early 1960's, I served with the Los Angeles Hebrew Mission, and one of my duties was to participate in street meetings in Jewish neighborhoods. Using a public-address system, I identified myself as a Hebrew Christian and then proceeded to give my testimony. I cannot tell you how often embittered Jews (many of them survivors of concentration camps), would accost me at the conclusion of a meeting and cast into my teeth the charge of "How could you, a Jew, ever choose to be a Christian? Don't you realize what the Christians did to our people in the Holocaust!"

Admittedly, these angry Jews had failed to distinguish between Christians and those Gentiles who really were responsible for the Holocaust. However, there is ample historic justification for Jews to associate Christians with those who repressed and tormented them from the Dark Ages on into the nineteenth century. The truth is, these persecutors were not Greeks nor Romans nor Nazis, they were Christians.

Early Christian Fathers Blame the Jews for Christ's Crucifixion

During the first few centuries of Christianity, Church fathers understandably blamed the Jews for Christ's crucifixion. The early Christian fathers claimed that God had forsaken the Jews. They taught that the "old Law" of the Jews was null and void, that the "new covenant" of Christianity had replaced it. This basically represented a doctrinal disagreement with the Jews rather than a physical persecution of them.

After the crucifixion, Christian and non-Christian Jews lived together in Jerusalem, though in a relative state of unease. When the Lord's brother, James the Just, was stoned to death in 62 A.D. by order of Ananus, the High Priest, Christian Jews fled the city. After the destruction of Jerusalem in 70 A.D. and the Roman dispersal, Jews were instrumental in fomenting persecution against the early Christians among both Romans and pagans. They were instrumental in the martyrdoms of Polycarp and many other Christian leaders in Asia minor, and they remained a strong voice against Christianity into the third century.

Medieval Christian Charges Against the Jews

By 1350, the Church's earlier anti-Judaism had become full-blown anti-Semitism, and added a litany of new charges against the Jews. They were accused of ritual murder, defilement of the Host, causing the Black Death by poisoning the water wells of England and Europe, and they were accused of conspiring to overthrow Christendom itself. Medieval art portrayed Jews as agents of Satan, having evil faces, horns, and tails. Sometimes the Devil himself might be seen in paintings and sculptures, riding on the backs of Jews. In a 15th century German woodcut, Jews are depicted as draining the blood from a Christian child, so as to make unleavened bread for their Passover.

All of this hatred was not only condoned by church leaders, but was in many cases instigated by them. For example, the Third Lateran Council

(1179) confirmed that "the Jew is the slave of the Christian," a concept originating with St. Augustine. Even Thomas Aquinas (1125-74) affirmed the legitimacy of holding the Jews in "perpetual servitude" for their crimes. Pope Innocent III (1198-1216) echoed the same sentiment when he declared:

> . . . the blasphemers of the Christian name [be] forced into servitude of which they made themselves deserving when they raised their sacrilegious hands against Him [Jesus] . . . [3]

The Doctrine of Servitus Judaeorum

By the 13th century the canonical legislation of the Roman Catholic Church was fully institutionalized, and the reprobate status of Jews was sealed by the doctrine of *Servitus Judaeorum* (the perpetual servitude of the Jews). In addition, the Fourth Lateran Council (1215) codified the Roman Church's determination to segregate Jews by requiring them to wear distinguishing clothing such as a conical hat, or a "Jew badge" (a yellow disc sewn onto the clothing). Mind you, this was eight hundred years before Nazi Germany, and it originated with the Church that was then claiming to act in the name of Jesus Christ, who died to save all men—including Jews.

A Comparison: Adolf Hitler and John Chrysostom

Let us, for a moment, use a contrast to demonstrate the historic persecution of Jews by Christians. First, listen to the words of Adolph Hitler; probably the most avid Jew-hater of the 20th century:

> I believe that I am acting in accordance with the will of the Almighty Creator: by defending myself

> against the Jew, I am fighting for the work of the Lord.[4]

Now listen to the words of one who was not only a Christian, but was also a church father, John Chrysostom (354-407), Bishop of Antioch:

> . . . the Synagogue is not only a whore house and a stage for actors, but a den of thieves and a refuge for wild beasts as well. . . . Jews have no conception of sacred matters and are in no way superior to goats and swine, leading debauched and gluttonous lives.[5]

By contrast, this particular statement from Hitler sounds almost benign. John Chrysostom was only one of several church fathers whose desire for vengeance sowed seeds of anti-Semitism in early Christianity. Ambros (339-397), Bishop of Milan, justified the destruction of a synagogue as appropriate action against "the enemies of Christ." Cyril (376-444), Patriarch of Alexandria, incited a mob against Jews, and in 415 brought about their expulsion from that city. Pope Innocent III, had this to say about Jews:

> The Jews, like Cain, are doomed to wander the earth as fugitives and vagabonds, and their faces are covered with shame.[6]

Pope Eugenius IV issued the following edict in 1442:

> We decree and order that from now on, and for all time, Christians shall not eat or drink with Jews, not admit them to feasts, nor cohabit with them, nor bathe with them. Christians shall not allow Jews to hold civil honors over Christians, or to exercise public office in the state.[7]

Does all of this sound like Nazi Germany in the 1930's? Even the most famous church father, St. Augustine (354-430), Bishop of Hippo, stated that the Jews ". . . can never grasp the meaning of the Holy Scriptures and will forever bear the guilt for the death of Jesus."[8] Regarding this anti-Semitism, Catholic historian, Edward Flannery, wrote that Innocent III and Henry II, Gregory VII and Henry VI, Thomas Aquinas, Dante and St. Francis of Assisi were all responsible to greater or lessor degrees for:

> . . . the age of anti-Jewish hecatombs [the slaughter of 100 victims], expulsions, calumnious myths, auto-da-fe [burning at the stake], the ghetto and many other hardships visited upon the Jews.[9]

Martin Luther's Anti-Semitism

Not only was anti-Semitism present in the Catholic Church, but also it was espoused by the founder of Protestantism himself, Martin Luther (1483-1546):

> . . . all their [the Jews] cash and jewels and silver and gold be taken from them and that their synagogues or schools be set on fire, that their houses be broken up and destroyed . . . and they be put under a roof or stable like gypsies . . . in misery and captivity as they incessantly complain to God about us [Christians].[10]

Such a vitriolic pronouncement would do honor to any member of the Nazi Party, yet it came not only from a Christian, but from a *great* Christian reformer. Still, it must be pointed out that Luther had had high hopes for Jewish conversions, once the Reformation had gotten under way. But when conversions failed to materialize, Luther became embittered against the Jews. Even in his waning years, he still harbored antagonism toward them, as evidenced when he wrote:

> If a Jew, not converted at heart, were to ask for baptism at my hands, I would take him on the bridge, tie a stone around his neck, and hurl him into the river; for these wretches are wont to make jest of our religion.[11]

Jews Slain by the Crusaders

Beyond all of this, was the slaughter of 10,000 Jews in France and Germany during the summer of 1096 by the crusaders. They were on their way to Palestine to wrest the sepulcher of Jesus from Muslim invaders. Godfrey Bouillon, the leader of this first crusade, swore to avenge the blood of Christ on Israel, and ". . . leave no single member of the Jewish race alive."

When Bouillon arrived in Palestine, he burned the synagogue of Jerusalem to the ground, with the worshippers still inside. Also, there was a second crusade in 1146, and although it was much less violent than the first, hundreds of Jewish lives were still lost.

The Decisions of Christian Councils

Finally, whenever the Roman Catholic Church convened a council, it frequently spelled bad news for the Jews. In the sixth century, the Synod of Orleans forbade Jews from employing Christians as servants. Further, Jews were forbidden to show themselves on the streets during Passion Week.

Also, in the seventh century, the Church ordered all copies of the Talmud burned. In addition, at this same time, the Synod of Clermont disqualified Jews from holding public office. Finally, in the thirteenth century, the Synod of Vienna outlawed Jews from ever discussing religion with Christians.

Spain's Edict of Expulsion

But perhaps the most flagrant example of anti-Semitism prior to Nazi Germany, occurred in the Middle Ages in Spain. On January 2, 1492, seven months before Columbus sailed on his discovery of America, King Ferdinand and Queen Isabella signed the "Edict of Expulsion," which banished all Jews (over 150,000 of them) from Spain, despite the fact that Jews had been a major part of the population there for at least 600 years. The sole justification for this expulsion was the assertion that Jewish presence was a serious spiritual threat to Spanish Christians.

The Spanish Inquisition Persecuted the Jews

In addition, between 1480 and 1834, the Spanish Inquisition tortured, then burned at the stake, over 100,000 Jews as "heretics." All this was done in the name of Jesus and Christianity. Admittedly, the idea of an inquisition did not originate with Spain, but hundreds of years earlier with St. Augustine. He provided the Spanish inquisitors with an advance justification for their cruelty, when he said:

> . . . "moderate persecution" (*tempereta severitas*) was permissible for turning heretics back to the straight path.[12]

Deuteronomy 28 Promised Persecution

To any student of scripture, persecution of the Jews comes as no surprise. God Himself promised it. If you read the 28th chapter of Deuteronomy, you will clearly see this Divine edict. The first 14 verses contain blessings in every area of Jewish life, for all those who obey the commandments of God. But, beginning at verse 15, all of the preceding blessings are inverted and become promised curses upon those who do not observe and keep God's commandments. One of these curses is persecution.

This persecution has certainly come to pass. However, should it come from those who call Jesus Lord and Savior? This same Jesus who wept over Jerusalem? Obviously it should not.

Rather, we as Christians, should pray for the Jews, and live Godly lives before them. We should live lives that demonstrate to these ancient people of the Book that our Lord and Savior is first and foremost a God of love. Thus, before He becomes a God of judgment, by reason of man's disbelief and disobedience, He is first and foremost a God of love.

Unfortunately, anti-Semitism will be with the Jews until Jesus Himself returns to reveal his Messianic presence to His disbelieving people. But until that time comes, let anti-Semitism emanate from the godless Gentiles, not from those who are followers of Christ.

6

Why Jews Don't Accept Jesus as the Son of God

In a 17th Century poem by Andrew Marvel, a man is attempting to woo a woman. He uses the argument that if only they had enough time for his courting and her coyness, she might refuse his advances ". . . till the conversion of the Jews." Interesting, is it not, that even in old English poetry, there existed the recognition that Jewish conversion to Christianity was one of the great improbables of this life. Most Christians would agree, without being able to put their finger on the *reason* for such Jewish aversion to Jesus.

The Jewish Shema

What, then, is the reason? Primarily, it's because Jesus claimed to be co-equal with God ("I and my Father are one"). Such a theological concept has always created an enormous problem for Jews, for it violates their belief that there is only one God. Judaism, unlike some branches of Christianity, has never convened ecclesiastical councils to determine doctrines and dogmas. However, there is one credo which has been the cornerstone of Judaism for over three thousand years. Originally, it made Israel different from all the nations surrounding it. This credo was a unique concept of God, for it declared that there is one and only one God (this in contrast to the pantheon of gods worshiped by those in neighboring lands). This Jewish credo is found in Deuteronomy 6:4: "Hear, O Israel: The LORD our God is one LORD."

This dogma of Judaism, called the *Shema* (the first word of the declaration), was and is universally accepted by all Jews, regardless of denomination. Among all "orthodox" and "conservative" Jewish males, the *Shema* must be recited both morning and evening. So sacred is this confession to Jews that the pious in Israel have always sought to die with it upon their lips. This has been true down through the ages, even to the Holocaust death camps, where Jews who were being put to death recited the *Shema* in their last moments on earth.

Admittedly the *Shema* is not part of the original Ten Commandments; however, Jesus Himself not only considered it to be a de facto commandment of God but the most important one. In Mark 12:28, 29, a scribe asks Christ, "Which is the first commandment of all" [first in importance]. Jesus replies, "The first of all the commandments is: Hear O Israel: the Lord our God is one Lord. . . ."

With this in mind, consider Jewish reaction to orthodox Christianity's doctrine of the Trinity. It asserts that there is one God, but that one God is manifested in three persons: a God the Father, and a God the Son, and a God the Holy Ghost. To Jews, this says that there are three Gods, not one. This is a concept antithetical to the very foundation upon which Judaism stands. No matter how painstakingly, an orthodox Christian may try to explain the Trinity to a Jew (assuming that one can logically explain it at all), the idea is absolutely untenable to him.

The Term Elohim

But is it possible that this basic tenet of Judaism has been misunderstood by its adherents for over 3000 years, and that in fact, it is in total agreement with the concept of the plurality of the one God? Look again at the *Shema*: "Hear, O Israel: The LORD our God [*Elohim*] is one [*echod*] LORD." (Deuteronomy 6:4).

The two words here that are crucial to understanding exactly what is revealed in this scripture, are *Elohim* and *echod*. The "im" ending on *Elohim* makes it a plural noun, and thus, it should correctly be rendered "Gods." This is exactly what one finds in over two hundred places throughout the Old Testament, where *elohim* often refers to the pagan gods of the gentiles. For example in Exodus 20:3 it says: "Thou shalt have no other gods [elohim] before me."

However, where *Elohim* refers to the God of Israel, it has typically been translated in the singular, as in Deuteronomy 6:5: "And thou shalt love the LORD thy God [*Elohim*] with all thy heart, and with all thy soul, and with all thy might."

Simply stated, you can't have it both ways. You can't say that *Elohim* is both singular and plural. It's like saying that "He has on one *shoe*" and also saying that "He has on two *shoe*." It just doesn't work. Despite this fact, Jewish translators have always rendered *Elohim* "God" rather than "Gods," as the spelling demands.

Hundreds of years ago, a rabbi named Simion Ben Joachi was meditating upon the word *Elohim* when he suddenly grasped a profound truth about it. He said:

> Come see the mystery of the word ELOHIM: There are three degrees, and each degree is by itself alone, and yet they are all one, and joined together in one, and are not divided from each other.[1]

Have Jewish translators persisted in rendering *Elohim* as singular in order to perpetuate the concept that God is one in the absolute sense? If so, then how would they explain the biblical use of plural pronouns which refer to God? In all of the following examples the emphasis is mine:

> Let *us* make man in *our* image after *our* likeness (Genesis 1:26).
>
> And the Lord God [*Elohim*] said, Behold, the man [Adam] is become as one of *us* to know good and evil: . . . (Genesis 3:22).
>
> Go to, let *us* go down, and there confound their language, that they may not understand one another's speech (Genesis 11:7).
>
> Also I heard the voice of the Lord, saying, Whom shall I send, and who will go for *us*? . . . (Isaiah 6:8).

In a Jewish translation of the Pentateuch entitled *The Torah, A Modern Commentary*, there is a section called "Gleaning" following each chapter. Here are presented a variety of commentaries by various Jewish scholars on difficult or controversial verses in each chapter. The "let *us* make man in *our* image" of Genesis 1:26 is commented upon by Franz Rosenzweig, a renowned Jewish intellectual of the early twentieth century. Regarding the use of the plural "us" and "our," Rosenzweig said:

> As long as God is still creating, He does not in fact say "I," He says "We," an absolute, all-inclusive term which does not refer to an *I* outside the self but is the plural of all-encompassing majesty. It is an impersonal *I*, an *I* that does not face another *Thou*, that does not reveal anything but lives, like the metaphysical God of precreation, only in itself.[2]

Other Evidence Which Shows the Plurality of God

Now to many this may sound like lofty biblical erudition, but it also sounds like an equivocation aimed at sweeping aside the obvious—that there is something pluralistic in God's nature. Jewish insistence that God is one in the absolute sense flies in the face of all the plural pronouns referring to Him. But there is even more evidence to support the plurality of God's nature.

Consider the other crucial word in the *Shema*, "*echod*" (one). There are two words in Hebrew denoting "one." *Echod* certainly means one, but not in the absolute sense. You might use *echod* to talk about "one" dozen eggs. Yes, it is only *one* dozen, but there are twelve eggs—not one. You find this use of *echod* in Genesis 2:24:

> Therefore shall a man leave his father and his mother, and shall cleave unto his wife: and they shall be one [echod] flesh.

One flesh, yes, but two people involved; like the dozen eggs which are considered as one. Had Moses wanted to convey in the *Shema* the concept that God is one in the absolute, solitary sense, he would have chosen the Hebrew word for "one" which denotes exactly that—*yâchîyd*. Look, for example, at Genesis 22:2:

> And he [God] said [to Abraham], Take thou thy son, thine only [*yâchîyd*] son Isaac, whom thou lovest, and get thee into the land of Moriah; and offer him there for a burnt offering . . ."

Considering the scriptural support presented here in defense of the plural nature of God, it seems illogical for Jews to reject Jesus as the Son of God. So, why then, did Jewish translators use the Hebrew plural noun for God in a singular form? Because though grammar correctly said one thing, Jewish tradition insisted upon something entirely different, and as we now know, tradition won out.

Is there perhaps an old adage that addresses this unfortunate Jewish reluctance to accept what is obvious biblical truth? Yes, there is, and it goes like this: "Don't confuse me with the facts; I've already made up my mind."

7

Why Jews Rejected Jesus as Their Messiah

Jesus Failed to Fulfill Jewish Messianic Expectations

There are many reasons given as to why the Jews in Jesus' day rejected Him as their long-awaited Messiah. One is that He claimed to be the Son of God, making Himself co-equal with God. Another is that He exercised the Divine prerogative of forgiving sin. Still another is that He said the Law no longer applied because He Himself was the fulfillment of that Law.

There are other, non-religious reasons why the Jews rejected Jesus. It is interesting to note, however, that while the suggested bases for Jewish rejection of Jesus as the Messiah during His lifetime focused on theological reasons, in fact, the primary reasons for His rejection actually were secular.

In a word, Jesus failed to fulfill Jewish Messianic expectations—expectations that had to do with earth rather than with heaven. These expectations were,

1. the destruction of the power of Rome over Jewish life in Palestine;

2. the overthrow of the Herodian monarchy and its being replaced by the Davidic dynasty with Messiah sitting on the throne;

3. the in-gathering of the dispersed and exiled Jews back to Palestine from around the world; and

4. the establishing of Israel in peace and safety in its own land.

Since none of this came to pass during Jesus' life, from a Jewish perspective, there was every reason to doubt His Messianic claims. Keep in mind that even the Lord's own disciples showed disappointment at His failure to exercise His Messianic power when the Jews arrested Him and brought Him before the Sanhedrin. At the same time, Christ's disciples physically abandoned Him out of fear and because He would not fight back. And when the Lord was nailed to the cross, His disciples had all of their belief in His Divinity crushed. After all, could the Romans, who were mere men, kill Christ if He were really God? Even after his resurrection, when Jesus told Mary Magdalene to tell His disciples the good news, scripture says that they did not believe her.

Therefore, it is not too difficult to understand the disappointment felt by the general Jewish population. Since life for them had not changed one iota during Jesus' three-year ministry, His claim to be the Messiah was regarded as nothing short of boasting—they perceived Him as another false messiah in Israel's long history of false prophets.

The Scriptural Standard for Measuring a Prophet's Authenticity

For fifteen hundred years the Book of Deuteronomy had given the Jews a yardstick for measuring the authenticity of a prophet's words. Deuteronomy 18:22, 23 states that if a prophet predicts something, and in the course of time, the prediction fails to come to pass, Israel was to totally disregard any future prophecies from that person.

Even Gamaliel, a teacher of the Law, warned the governing council and the high priest against harming Peter and the other disciples of Jesus for preaching. In Acts 5:33-39 Gamaliel says that if the disciples are wrong, then they will fade away and nothing more will be heard of them. However, if they are right, if Jesus is in fact the Messiah, and all messianic expectation comes to pass, then the council should give up its persecution of these people because they would be fighting against God Himself.

But Israel's world remained unchanged during Jesus' lifetime, and in fact, even got much worse. Less than forty years after Jesus' crucifixion, Titus and his Roman legions descended upon Jerusalem, utterly destroyed the city, and scattered the Jews to the far corners of the world.

Messianic Expectations to Be Fulfilled in a Second Advent

Contrast this with the Messianic expectation that the Jews would be gathered back to Palestine, and Israel would be established in safety and prominence in its own land:

> And my people shall dwell in a peaceable habitation, and in sure dwellings, and in quiet resting places (Isaiah 32:18).

Also,

> And he shall set up an ensign for the nations, and shall assemble the outcasts of Israel, and gather together the dispersed of Judah from the four corners of the earth (Isaiah 11:12).

Beyond this, the Jews of Jesus' day were looking forward to the Messiah's coming, for then would be fulfilled the prophecy that all natural violence would cease:

> And the wolf shall dwell with the lamb, and the leopard shall lie down with the kid; and the calf and the young lion and the fatling together; and a little child shall lead them.
>
> . . . And the lion shall eat straw like the ox.
>
> And the sucking child shall play on the hole of the asp, and the weaned child shall put his hand on the cockatrice's den.
>
> They shall not hurt nor destroy in all My holy mountain: . . . (Isaiah 11:6-9).

One may well ask why the Jews couldn't discern between the first and the second coming of the Messiah. Simply stated, it was because none of the prophets who wrote about the coming Messiah, and how the world would be radically changed because of His coming, specifically stated that there would be two advents, not just one. None of these writers: Isaiah, Daniel, Micah and others, specifically identified the 2000-year era that would intervene between the Messiah's earthly advent, "For unto us a child is born . . ." (Isaiah 9:6) and his future millennial reign:

> And it shall come to pass in the end days, that the mountain of the Lord's house shall be established in the top of the mountains . . . and all nations shall flow unto it.
>
> . . . and they shall beat their swords into plowshares, and their spears into pruninghooks . . . neither shall they learn war anymore (Isaiah 2:2, 4).

It was as though these holy prophets were looking through a kaleidoscope, seeing all of the coming Messianic events but describing them in only a single dimension; without specifically identifying the time period that would separate them.

Why Many First-Century Jews Were Converted to Jesus

So, how then, does one explain why so many Jews of the first Century embraced Jesus as their Messiah? It seems that what was of primary importance to these early converts was not national fulfillment, but personal salvation.

These Christian Jews already knew that Jewish Messianic expectations were not going to be fulfilled in their lifetime; particularly in view of the events of 70 A.D. But that didn't matter. What was important was that these early Jewish Christians found the balm for their troubled souls—a balm that years of ritual, prayer, and temple sacrifice had been unable to provide. And that's what it's really all about—a personal relationship with God, rather than a national one.

Many Jews Today Still Look for the Messiah's Coming

Many Jews today still look for the coming of a personal Messiah. Those who don't, have spiritually impoverished themselves. Abraham Ezra Millgram says:

> Without wishing to impugn in the slightest degree, then, the legitimacy of any Jew who earnestly seeks to find God, it is difficult, in the light of this all-pervasive belief in the eventual coming of the Messiah, to see how one can be a believing Jew while abandoning this doctrine.[1]

Yes, Jews have long rejected Jesus as their Messiah. But the day is coming when these disbelieving, ancient people of God will indeed say, "Blessed is He who comes in the name of the Lord."

8

A Jewish Paradox

Jews and Jesus are not topics generally discussed in the same breath, yet there exists today a paradox between two separate groups of Jews regarding both their differing attitudes toward the historic Jesus and their contrasting interpretations of their own Jewish religion.

Strangely enough, the orthodox Jews, who studiously ignore Jesus, are closer to Him theologically than are the reform and reconstructionist Jews (both groups hereafter referred to as "liberal" Jews). The liberal Jews not only freely discuss Jesus, but also, in some respects, hold Him in considerable esteem.

Keep in mind that orthodox Jews reject Jesus on every count: as an historic personage, as Messiah, and most certainly as Son of God. In fact, they cannot even bring themselves to say His name aloud. On the other hand, liberal Jews harbor no such animosity toward Christ. Their position on the historic Jesus is reflected in the words of no less a Jewish luminary than Albert Einstein. The following excerpt is from a personal interview with him which appeared in the *Saturday Evening Post:*

> ***Question:*** To what extent are you influenced by Christianity?
>
> ***Answer:*** As a child I received instruction both in the Bible and in the Talmud. I am a Jew, but I am enthralled by the luminous figure of the Nazarene.
>
> ***Question:*** Do you accept the historical existence of Jesus?
>
> ***Answer:*** Unquestionably! No one can read the Gospels without feeling the actual presence of Jesus. His personality pulsates in every word. No myth is filled with such life.[1]

With this background in mind, consider now the paradox and the three fundamental religious differences existing between orthodox and liberal Jews which, strangely enough, place the orthodox Jew, the least kindly disposed toward Jesus, closer to Him theologically.

The Inspiration and Permanence of the Law of Moses

The first of these differences concerns the Divine inspiration of the Law of Moses and its permanence.

During His lifetime, Jesus taught that the Law given to Moses was the rock-solid, authoritative Word of God, and nothing would ever change it except for its being fulfilled. Jesus declared this in no uncertain terms:

> . . . Till heaven and earth pass, one jot or one tittle shall in no wise pass from the Law, till all be fulfilled (Matthew 5:18).

Orthodox Jews, the very ones who would put as much distance between themselves and Jesus as possible, agree wholeheartedly with His position on the Law. Moses Maimonides, perhaps the most important Jewish philosopher at the end of the Dark Ages, codified thirteen articles of faith which every Jew must acknowledge if he wishes to share in the "world to come." Articles VIII and IX of that code state:

> I believe with perfect faith that the whole Law, now in our possession, is the same that was given to Moses our teacher . . . I believe with perfect faith that this law will not be changed, and that there will never be another Law from the Creator.[2]

Now contrast this orthodox article of faith with the position held by liberal Jews. In Pittsburgh in 1885, a symposium of reform rabbis met to draw up a declaration of principles which would state their theological position relative to the Law and to the many Jewish traditions which were considered de facto law. Regarding Jesus' and orthodox Jews' position on the Law, Article III of the Reform Declaration of Principles states:

> We recognize in the Mosaic legislation a system of training the Jewish people for its mission during its national life in Palestine, and today we accept as binding only its moral laws and maintain only such ceremonials as elevate and sanctify our lives, but reject all such as are not adapted to the views and habits of modern civilization.[3]

Please note that there exists in this article of faith an implicit suggestion that as civilization's "views" and "habits" change, so will liberal Judaism's interpretation and adherence to Mosaic law. Such a position is certainly light years away from that held by Jesus and orthodox Jews.

The Doctrine of Resurrection

A second essential difference between orthodox and liberal Jews, and one which again puts Jesus and the orthodox side by side, is the doctrine of resurrection. It is interesting to note that most non-orthodox Jews view resurrection as a Christian doctrine—not as a Jewish one. They associate it entirely with the "claimed" bodily resurrection of Jesus, totally ignoring the fact that their own prophet, Daniel, wrote of it as early as the sixth century B.C.:

> . . . many of them that sleep in the dust of the earth shall awake, some to everlasting life, and some to shame and everlasting contempt (Daniel 12:2).

Certainly Jesus Himself espoused this doctrine, for He declared:

> Marvel not at this: for the hour is coming, in which all that are in the graves shall hear his [God's] voice,
>
> And shall come forth; they that have done good, unto the resurrection of life; and they that have done evil, unto the resurrection of damnation (John 5:28, 29).

In complete accord with Jesus' teaching on bodily resurrection is the position of the orthodox Jews. In Maimonides' thirteenth article of faith we find the following:

> I believe with perfect faith that there will be a resurrection of the dead at the time when it shall please the Creator, blessed be His name . . .[4]

Now compare the biblical position concerning resurrection held by Jesus and orthodox Jews with that of liberal Jews. In the Reform Declaration of Principles, one finds article VII, which states:

> We reject as ideas not rooted in Judaism the belief both in bodily resurrection and in Gehenna and Eden (Hell and Paradise) as abodes for everlasting punishment and reward.[5]

Interesting, is it not, how close Jesus and orthodox Jews are in theology, and how much distance liberal Judaism has placed between itself and Old Testament teaching?

The Coming of the Messiah

The final, primary difference between Jesus and the orthodox Jews on one hand, and liberal Jews on the other, is one that strikes at the heart of historic Judaism—the coming of the Messiah. Not only does the Bible, history, and the personal faith of hundreds of millions of Christians for almost two thousand years, attest to the fact that the Messiah has already come, but also the fact that Jesus of Nazareth was, and is, that Messiah. Certainly Jesus Himself declared this openly to Jerusalem's high priest:

> And the high priest stood up in the midst, and asked Jesus, saying, Answerest thou nothing? What is it which these witness against thee?
>
> But he held his peace, and answered nothing. Again the high priest asked him, and said unto him, Art thou the Christ [Messiah], the Son of the Blessed?
>
> And Jesus said, *I am*; and ye shall see the Son of man sitting on the right hand of power, and coming

> in the clouds of heaven (Mark 14:60-62, emphasis mine).

In his book, *Messianic Speculation in Israel*, Rabbi Abba Silver makes the point that the pious in Israel have always longed for, and awaited expectantly, the coming of their Messiah; the one who would deliver them from all national privation and persecution. Certainly this is what Article XII of Maimonides' Articles of Faith declares, which orthodox Jews recite every day:

> I believe with perfect faith in the coming of the Messiah, and though he tarry, I will wait daily for his coming.[6]

Now, contrast this with the position held by liberal Jews, who have no such hope. To them the Messiah is not a person but rather a period of time; a world condition in which Utopia has finally become a reality. This belief is clearly stated in Article V of their Declaration of Principles:

> We recognize in the modern era of universal culture of hearts and intellect, the approaching of the realization of Israel's great messianic hope for the establishment of the kingdom of truth, justice, and peace among all men. We consider ourselves no longer a nation but a religious community and therefore expect neither a return to Palestine, nor a sacrificial worship under the administration of the sons of Aaron, nor the restoration of any of the laws concerning the Jewish state.[7]

This is the sad end at which liberal Jews have arrived in abandoning their belief in a personal Messiah. This ancient hope they have exchanged for the forlorn hope that man, through his own feeble efforts, can bring about a messianic kingdom of peace among all men.

A personal Messiah, a man of flesh and blood (as was Jesus at His first advent), is what all of ancient Judaism looked for. Jewish writer, David Barron, says that the very first prophecy regarding the Messiah speaks of a personal one:

> With regard to this prophecy [Genesis 49:10] the first thing I want to point out is that all antiquity agrees in interpreting it of a personal Messiah. This is the view of the Septuagint, the Targumin of Onkelos, Yonathan, the Zohar, the ancient book of "Bereshith Rabbi," and among modern commentators even Rashi, who says, ". . . until Shiloh come, that is King Messiah, whose is the Kingdom."[8]

Thus, one can easily see the paradox in which orthodox Jews, who refuse to consider or even to mention the name of Jesus, are closer to Him in spirit and in mind, than are liberal Jews, who not only openly discuss Jesus, but also hold Him in some measure of esteem. They see Him as a wise teacher, or at least as a good-intentioned Jew. Yet, these same liberal Jews are the ones who are farthest from His teachings and theology.

Reflections on Traditions and Dogma

Two truths emerge out of this paradox which are applicable to everyone, Jew and non-Jew alike. First, people should realize that to perpetuate a particular religious attitude or practice, simply because it is a tradition, is to ignore the fact that "tradition" has to do with continuity, not with truth. Unfortunately, there exists in the human heart, a tendency to deem as being "true" something which has been only traditional. Traditions are easily born. As the old adage says, "Do a thing twice and it becomes a habit; do it three times and it becomes a tradition." The orthodox aversion to the historic Jesus is merely a tradition. Certainly it has no basis in the Old Testament. In fact, quite the opposite is true with regard to the prophetic Messiahship of Jesus.

Secondly, a religious belief, or even an entire set of religious dogma, is not necessarily true simply because a group of adherents formally declare it to be so. Writing it down on a scroll doesn't necessarily make it a thus-saith-the-Lord pronouncement. For liberal Jews to pick and choose what is currently applicable to them and what is not regarding God's Law, is analogous to a group of American citizens formally declaring that the Internal Revenue Act no longer applies to them.

Therefore, as in the case of the orthodox Jews' traditional rejection of Jesus, and in the case of the liberal Jews' self-declared theology, neither has a biblical foundation. Both are the products of human reason—not Divine revelation. Perhaps Scripture says it best:

> Trust in the Lord with all thine heart; and lean not unto thine own understanding (Proverbs 3:5).

9

Jewish Attitudes Toward Sin

Many religious Jews would agree with Christians concerning doctrines such as the coming of the Messiah, the resurrection of the dead, and the final judgment of God. Some would even agree on the source of sin—man's propensity toward it. However, it is over the perception of sin itself and repentance, that Jews and Christians sharply diverge.

"Original Sin" Not a Jewish Belief

Both orthodox and liberal Jews believe that at birth, God gives man a pure and holy soul, and though man possesses a latent possibility toward good *or* evil, his inclination is stronger toward good. Judaism maintains that man starts life with a plus, not with a minus. It does not believe in an inherited sin from Adam.

The concept of original sin is almost completely absent from rabbinical writings and from the Mishnah (the compilation of the Oral Law). Nowhere in the Old Testament are the Hebrews ordered to atone for an inherited burden of guilt. Sacrifices were never offered in the temple for original sin, nor was there any ritual of propitiation prescribed for it.

"Original Sin" a Late-Adopted Christian Doctrine

The doctrine of "original sin" did not exist in the early Christian church. It came much later—"original sin" did not even appear as an official Church doctrine until declared so by the Council of Trent (1545-1563). Of course, in his epistles, Paul says that we are all inheritors of Adam's sin of rebellion against God, but "original sin," as a doctrine of orthodox Christianity, did not occur until over fifteen hundred years after Paul's writings. Today some Christian faiths believe that they are the inheritors of Adam's sin, but such a doctrine is totally foreign to Judaism.

Referring to man's having a pure soul at birth, Rabbi Abba Hillel Silver said:

> The authoritative teaching of Judaism was and remains: "My God, the soul which Thou hast placed in me is pure. Thou hast fashioned it in me. Thou didst breathe it into me."[1]

Can One "Think" a Sin?

Not only do Jews deny the concept of original sin, they reject the idea that a person can *think* sinful thoughts. Here again, Jews and Christians diverge. For example, Jesus says:

> But I say unto you that whosoever looketh on a woman to lust after her hath committed adultery with her already in his heart (Matthew 5:28).

This is certainly meaningful to Christians, but is meaningless to Jews. In Judaism, one cannot *think* a sin, one can only *do* a sin. Of course the tenth commandment of Moses, ". . . thou shalt not covet thy neighbour's wife . . ." (Exodus 20:17), must be judiciously disposed of in order to hold to such a position.

Rabbi Isaac Meyer Wise, one of the founders of Reform Judaism, felt that sin actually served a positive end in that an individual has only to overcome it (by his own effort, of course) to lift himself one rung higher on the ladder toward becoming a better person. It seems that the only category of sin upon which Christians and Jews *do* agree is the one covering sins of commission and sins of omission. But as already mentioned, these are actions, not mere thoughts.

Is It the Body or the Soul that Sins?

One of the areas regarding sin over which the ancient rabbis wrestled was whether the body or the soul actually does the sinning. The following rabbinic homily demonstrates their problem:

> A man dies, and his soul goes to heaven. God says to the soul: "Why did you sin?" The soul replies, "Me? Why since I have been here I have flown around heaven as innocent as a bird. How have I sinned?" God then speaks to the man's body: "Why did you sin?" The body replies, "Listen, since the soul left me I have lain here like a fallen rock. How could I be the one who sinned?"

Another rabbinic homily shows how one's responsibility for sinning is largely a question of perception and interpretation:

> An orchard owner leaves on a trip and puts two men in charge of his prize fig tree. One of the men is blind and the other lame. After the owner departs,

the lame man says, "My, do those figs look delicious!" The blind man replies, "I will tell you what, I will put you on my shoulders and you can guide us to the fig tree."

So they agree, and during the next several days they eat all of the figs. Then the owner returns to find his prize figs gone. He confronts the two men: "Who ate my figs?" "Why ask me," says the lame man, "I cannot walk." "Well do not ask me," says the blind man, "I cannot see."

The *Yetzer Ha-ra:* Inclination to Sin

Although the ancient rabbis were never able to agree on whether it was the body or the soul that sinned, they certainly were in accord as to the source of sin. In fact, Christian theology heartily concurs on this point. In Genesis 8:21, the last half of the verse says, ". . . for the imagination of man's heart is evil from his youth; . . ." The word "imagination" in Hebrew is *yetzer* and means "inclination," "device," "purpose."

There are actually two *yetzers: yetzer ha-ra* (the evil *Yetzer*) and *yetzer tob* (the good *Yetzer*). It was the *yetzer ha-ra* with which the rabbis were concerned, recognizing that it was an evil which fueled man's lusts, drives, and desires. Of course this rabbinical perception of the cause of sin stands in direct contrast to the generally-accepted proposition in Judaism that man is basically good and that his behavior gravitates more toward *virtuous* actions than toward evil ones.

So concerned were the rabbis of old regarding the *yetzer ha-ra* within man, that they wrote many truisms to point out the imminent danger in giving place to these evil imaginations. Here are just a few examples of those rabbinic warnings. All of these examples are from *A Rabbinic Anthology:*

> This is the device of the evil *yetzer:* today it says do this; tomorrow it says do that, till at last it says, "worship an idol" and the man goes and does.
>
> The *yetzer* at first is weak as a woman; afterwards it becomes strong as a man.
>
> At first the evil *yetzer* is like a spider's thread, and at last it is like a rope of a ship.
>
> At first it [*yetzer ha-ra*] is a wayfarer and a lodger, at last it becomes master of the house.
>
> If a man indulges his *yetzer* in his youth it will be his ruler in his old age.

The rabbis agreed that the only effective remedy for the evil *yetzer* was the study of the Law. However, had these learned men read the epistles of Paul, they probably would have agreed with his argument, that the very prohibitions contained within the Law are what excite and stir up *yetzer ha-ra*. However, the rabbis could not determine whether the evil *yetzer* emanated from the soul or from the body.

Differing Beliefs on the Nature of Repentance

We have briefly examined the Jewish attitude toward the commission of sin and the source of sin. What remains to be seen is repentance for sin.

Consider this: some Christians believe that one must accept Jesus Christ as providing atonement for their sins before they can live righteous lives that are pleasing to God. Jews, on the other hand, believe that living the most moral and ethical life one can, plus atoning for accumulated yearly sin on the Day of Atonement, is what really pleases God.

To the Jew, atonement occurs once a year, every year, on the Day of Atonement. As a result, there is no need in Judaism for a Savior who came to earth to die once and for all as an everlasting atonement for men's sins. However, to the Christian, complete atonement occurred once two thousand years ago, never again to be repeated.

It would not be an exaggeration to say that modern-day Jews, particularly liberal ones, do not take atonement nearly as seriously as did the rabbis of old, who believed that sacrifice, restitution and apology were worthless expressions of atonement unless accompanied by ". . . a broken spirit: a broken and a contrite heart" (Psalms 51:17).

They also believed that confession counted for little in atoning for sin unless accompanied by genuine repentance. In other words, a firm resolve not to commit that sin again, should opportunity present itself. After all, they taught, God was far more ready to forgive than He was to judge. Rabbi Issi put it this way:

> God says to the Israelites, ". . . open to me my children the gate of repentance as minute as the eye of a needle, and I will open for you gates wide enough for carriages and wagons to enter through them."[3]

Targum Yoma (Targums were the translations of the books of the Hebrew Bible into Aramaic), commenting on the need for genuine repentance, said:

> . . . Sin offering and guilt offering and the Day of Atonement and death—all of them together do not expiate sin without repentance.[4]

Concerning atonement unaccompanied by a resolve to henceforth refrain from sin, Rabbi Bebai wrote:

> If a man holds an unclean thing in his hand, he may dip in all the seas of creation yet he will never become clean. Let him throw away the unclean thing and a very small amount of water will suffice.[5]

The really wonderful thing about genuine spiritual repentance is that it operates exactly opposite to our justice system here on earth. "He that covereth his sins shall not prosper: but whoso confesseth and forsaketh them shall have mercy" (Proverbs 28:13).

In our criminal justice system, if a man confesses his crime in a human tribunal, he is punished for that crime. But if he keeps his mouth shut, there is a good chance he may be acquitted. On the other hand, with God it is just the opposite: If a man does *not* confess his transgression he will surely be punished, yet if he confesses it to the Judge (God), he can be pronounced innocent and acquitted.

One final note on repentance needs to be made. The ancient rabbis believed that habitual lapses of uninterrupted sin bring a man to the point where the power to repent is taken from him by God. Still, the Lord is reluctant to do this—as evidenced by His patience with the generation of the Flood, with the builders of the tower of Babel, and with the inhabitants of Sodom. Even Pharaoh was allowed to repent five times before God had enough of Pharaoh's insincerity and consequently hardened his heart so that he could no longer repent.

The rabbis of old agreed that among the things God created for man, the Law was first, followed closely by "repentance." Why? Because God knew that man could not perfectly keep the Law and as a result would have to be punished. Repentance was man's only escape from Divine punishment.

Christians certainly have their share of promises in the New Testament regarding forgiveness of sin through the atoning blood of Christ Jesus. But long before there was a New Testament, Jews had their promises of forgiveness too:

> I, even I, am he who blotteth out thy transgression for mine own sake, and will not remember thy sins (Isaiah 43:25).

> Come now, and let us reason together, saith the Lord: though your sins be as scarlet, they shall be white as snow; though they be red like crimson, they shall be as wool (Isaiah 1:18).

> . . . for I will forgive their iniquity, and I will remember their sin no more (Jeremiah 31:34).

> As far as the east is from the west, so far hath he removed our transgressions from us (Psalms 103:12).

> . . . he [God] will have compassion upon us; . . . and thou wilt cast all their sins into the depths of the sea (Micah 7:19).

Christians certainly do not agree with much of the rabbinic theology presented here regarding sin. However, to use a popular phrase, we at least should "know where they're coming from" when Jews disagree with Christian concepts of sin.

10

Two Dates That Changed Judaism Forever

Monumentally significant in the history of the Jews are two dates: (1) 586 B.C., when Nebuchadnezzar destroyed the first temple and exiled the Jews to Babylon, and (2) 70 A.D., when Titus and his Roman legions destroyed the second temple and put Jerusalem to the torch. Both dates forever changed the traditional direction of religious Jews.

The Babylonian Captivity

The Oral Law Committed to Writing

During the Babylonian captivity, Jews, bereft of their temple and its ritual, were forced to reinterpret the Pentateuch (the five books of Moses) in light of their radically changed life-styles and circumstances in a foreign land. To do this they committed the Oral Law to writing, something unthinkable in the past. Tradition held that after receiving the written Law from God upon Sinai, Moses was also given the Oral Law, which he then taught to Joshua, thereby inaugurating a transmission by mouth of the Oral Law.

Exiled Jews claimed that proof of the existence of the Oral Law was to be found in Exodus 34:27, and thus it became their justification for the change:

> And the Lord said unto Moses, Write thou these words; for after the tenor [Hebrew *al-peh*, "by the mouth"] of these words I have made a covenant with thee and with Israel.

To fully appreciate the radical nature of this Jewish decision to reinterpret Torah, imagine if you will, 20,000 Christians being exiled to China from America. Upon arrival, they find that the Chinese government forbids the practice of their faith as they have known it. There is no baptizing allowed, nor observing of the sacraments, nor Christmas, nor Easter. Now suppose these Christians decide that to follow their faith they need to reinterpret not only the four gospels but also all of the epistles as well. As scriptural justification for such a radical change they cite Philippians 2:12:

> Wherefore, my beloved, as ye have always obeyed, not as in my presence only, but now much more in my absence, *work out your own salvation* with fear and trembling (emphasis mine).

Can you begin to understand how monumental the decision for these exiled Jews was to change what had always been considered sacrosanct and unchangeable? This Oral Law, this co-authoritative expansion of the Pentateuch, grew rapidly, and around 457 B.C. was taken back to Jerusalem by Ezra and a large company of Jews returning to their homeland.

The Founding of Synagogue Worship

There was also another change instituted during the Babylonian captivity. It was the founding of synagogue worship. This was not intended to be a substitute for the lost temple, but was rather to bring the exiled Jews together in one place and to be of one mind. This was to prevent losing touch with their Jewishness and with their Judaism. So, Ezra took back to Jerusalem not only the redacted Oral Law (known as the *Mishnah*) but also the practice of synagogue worship.

Scribes Become Spiritual Leaders

Once in Palestine, Ezra instituted a body of scribes who became known as "Men of the Great Assembly." These spiritual leaders represented the supreme legal authority for all Jewish people, both in and out of Judah. The scribes were able biblical scholars who were zealous of the written Law of Moses, but in light of their changed living circumstances they felt quite free to interpret and alter some of its outmoded regulations. Thus the *Mishnah* continued to be developed. In Matthew 15:2 and Mark 7:3-5 it is referred to as the "traditions of the elders."

Though the synagogue idea originated during the Babylonian captivity, it was the scribes—the Men of the Great Assembly—who really developed the synagogue. They made it an institution of the layman, whereas in contrast, the temple had always been the sole domain of the priests.

Eventually the "Great Assembly" died out and was replaced by the Sanhedrin with its upper and lower chambers. The upper house (priests and aristocrats) denied the validity of the written "Oral" Law whereas the lower house (those who inherited the oral traditions of the scribes) championed it. However, in 70 A.D., contention over the Oral Law ended with the destruction of the second temple, of the Sanhedrin, and of much of the Jewish adherence to the Law of Moses.

The Mishnah Gains Eminence with the Rise of the Rabbis

It was shortly after this that the *Mishnah* gained eminence over the Torah, and the rise of the rabbis occurred. It was the rabbis who determined that the Oral Law itself needed interpretation and thus was born the *Gemara*—volumes of rabbinic comments and interpretations of the *Mishnah*. This work of the rabbis began around 200 A.D. and was finished by about the year 500 A.D.

So intertwined and inseparable were the *Mishnah* and *Gemara* as codifications of *Halakhah* (the day-by-day walk in life), that they became known as the *Talmud*, and eventually became as authoritative in Judaism as was the Torah itself.

It is really the *Talmud* which draws the distinction between Judaism and the Hebrew religion. The Hebrew religion was the practice and observance of Mosaic Law prior to the destruction of the second temple. On the other hand, "Judaism" represents the belief and observances set forth in the *Talmud*.

The Talmud

As already mentioned, the *Talmud* has two parts: the *Mishnah*, which is the written text, and the *Gemara*, which comprises the thousands upon thousands of rabbinic commentaries regarding that text. The *Gemara* was divided into six major divisions and each of these had many subdivisions. For example, under the major division of "Damages," one finds ten tractates (rabbinic dissertations) dealing with subjects such as compensation for damages; one's responsibility toward a neighbor's property; and real estate (laws of tenantry, joint tenants, inheritance, and division of property). Also appearing are tractates on courts, punishment by "stripes," oaths, testimonies, and other legal considerations. There is little room for one's own private interpretation in Talmudic Judaism. Every aspect of a Jew's life was proscribed and regulated.

The compiling and codification of the *Gemara* took place at about the same time as the compilation of the New Testament. As Christianity claimed that the New Testament was more important than the Old Testament because the New was the fulfillment of the Old, so too did Jews claim that the *Talmud* was more important than the *Torah* with its outmoded and unfulfillable temple requirements. In a sense, the *Talmud* became the "gospel" for second century Jews.

A Contrast: Jewish Legalism and Christian Creedism

In the book, *Understanding the Talmud*, the author draws the following contrast between Judaism and Christianity:

> It is interesting to note that at the time the rabbis were developing the *Halakic* aspects of Judaism (thereby making Judaism an "action" religion filled

> with observances) the church fathers were developing the creeds of Christianity (thereby making Christianity a "faith" religion filled with articles of belief). Thus, the legalism of the rabbis was matched by the "creedalism" of the church fathers. . . .[1]

The Destruction of the Second Temple

The destruction of the first temple in 586 B.C. was devastating enough for the Jews, but its lasting effects were relatively short—less than a century.

Moral Deeds Substituted for Altar Sacrifices

However, with the destruction of the second temple in 70 A.D., the very soul was permanently torn out of Israel, including the loss of the altar of sacrifice, and atonement for sin. Access to God would never again be possible through animal blood atonement. Obviously a substitute for the loss of such sacrifices had to be found, and so it was. Hosea 6:6 became the scriptural justification for the substitutions that evolved:

> For I desired mercy, and not sacrifice; and the knowledge of God more than burnt offerings.

Rabbis enacted a system of moral deeds which substituted for altar sacrifices, and the phrase, "He who performs this or that act is considered to have brought a sacrifice," was coined. There are four categories of such substitutes: 1. tenets of Jewish faith, 2. ritual acts, 3. ethical deeds, and 4. events in one's personal life.

An example of the *first* category, "tenets of Jewish faith" is one's dedicated study of the Law. It is said that he who studies the Law is metaphorically rebuilding the temple. Also, he who busies himself with *Torah* is like a man tendering a burnt offering. Prayer, too, is considered a substitute for sacrifice. Hosea 14:2 states that "[We] will . . . render the calves of our lips." Repentance also is considered a substitute for sacrifice: "The sacrifices of God are a broken spirit: a broken and a contrite heart" (Psalms 51:17). This is understood to mean that if a man repents, it is accounted unto him as if he had gone up to Jerusalem and built the temple and the altar and offered thereon all the sacrifices ordained in the Torah.[2]

The *second* category, "ritual acts," substitutes the penitent sinner's own fat and blood as the sacrifice. This is accomplished through fasting. The one who is fasting prays thus:

> May it be Thy will to account my fat and blood which have been diminished as if I had offered them before Thee on the altar, and do Thou favor me.[3]

The *third* category, "ethical deeds," allows one to substitute *mitzvoth* (meritorious, virtuous acts) for sacrifice. For example, making certain that the poor's share in the harvest (Leviticus 23:22) and in other provisions is met, is equated with a man's having made his offering in the temple itself.

The *fourth* category, "events in one's personal life," considers such things as circumcision, feeding the poor at one's own table, and a person's own death as an offering of sacrifice.

Officiating Priests Replaced by Pious, Ordinary Men

Last of all, with the destruction of the temple, the officiating priests were replaced by pious, ordinary men. So complete was the transition from altar sacrifice to substitute sacrifice that Jews actually began criticizing the past centuries of traditional blood sacrifice. In support of this criticism, verses in Isaiah and Psalms were quoted as justification for the present system of substitutions:

> To what purpose is the multitude of your sacrifices unto me? saith the LORD: I am full of the burnt offerings of rams, and the fat of fed beasts; and I delight not in the blood of bullocks, or of lambs, or of he-goats (Isaiah 1:11).

Also,

> For thou desirest not sacrifice; else would I give it: thou delightest not in burnt offering (Psalms 51:16).

Two points need to be made here: (1) there is no authority from God that makes rabbinic comment and interpretation more authoritative than God's own revealed Word. Of course, Jews would argue that the "chain of tradition" (each generation's rabbis exercise authority which reaches all the way back to Moses) is a true and valid concept; (2) and that with the close of the Old and New Testament canons, post-biblical commentaries and interpretations of rabbis (albeit learned men) are nothing more than that—the writings of men and not of God.

However, despite the loss of the temple and altar, atonement for sin continues to be available today to all Jews through their observance of the substitute sacrifices. Admittedly this is not the Judaism of Moses, Joshua, David, and others, but it is nonetheless Judaism as it exists today.

11

Bias in Jewish Bible Translations

There have been many translations of the Bible over the centuries. Some of the most significant are: (1) the "Septuagint" from Hebrew to Greek in the third century B.C.; (2) St. Jerome's "Vulgate" Bible from Hebrew to Latin in the fourth century A.D.; (3) John Wycliffe's translation from Latin to English in the fourteenth century; (4) William Tyndale's translation from Hebrew and Greek into English in the sixteenth century; and (5) the King James translation in the seventeenth century.

There are many more translations both before and after the King James which could be mentioned, but suffice it to say that whenever you read a translation of any book, you are dependent upon the translator for an honest, unbiased, and contextually-correct reproduction. Such a dependency is, of course, not necessary where the writer is both author and translator, as in the case of O.E. Rolvaag's *Giants in the Earth*, originally written in

Norwegian and then translated into English by Rolvaag himself.

Examples of Unintentional Translation Errors

With regard to translations of the Bible, there are two basic errors which can occur: (1) unintentional mistakes and (2) deliberate distortion resulting from a traditional bias held by the translator.

For example, an unintentional error in St. Jerome's Latin "Vulgate" occurs in Exodus 34:29, where the translator rendered "skin of his [Moses'] face" as "his face was horned" (horns in Latin are *cornuta*). There was no deception intended here; however, it did cause Michelangelo years later to give his statue of Moses *cornuta*—horns on his head.

Another example of innocent error is found in Myles Coverdale's 1537 translation known as the "Treacle" Bible. This error occurred as a result of Jeremiah 8:22 being rendered as: "is there no treacle in Gilead?" instead of "is there no balm in Gilead?" A treacle is actually an antidote against the poisonous bite of a wild animal. Certainly this is not in the context of the verse.

Examples of Errors Based on Traditional Biases

Unintentional error in translation is understandable, but deliberate error based upon traditional bias is unconscionable. A translator may not be able to bring complete objectivity to his work, but he should at least be honest. This has not always been true of scholars who translated the Old Testament, or the Torah, from Hebrew into English.

Genesis 1:2

For example, Genesis 1:2 in the King James translation says:

> And the earth was without form, and void; and darkness was upon the face of the deep. And the Spirit of God moved upon the face of the waters.

The same passage in *The Torah, A Modern Commentary* (for Jewish readers) states:

> The earth being unformed and void, with darkness over the surface of the deep and a *wind* from God *sweeping* over the water (emphasis mine).

Two pairs of words need to be examined here: "Spirit" and "moved" in the King James, and "wind" and "sweeping" in the Jewish translation. Neither "moved" nor "sweeping" carry the primary meaning of *ráchaph*—a Hebrew prime root denoting "brood." It is interesting that of the nineteen words in the Hebrew lexicon of the Old Testament denoting "move," "moved," or "to move," Genesis 1:2 is the only place where *ráchaph*, "brood," occurs, and only once in the entire Old Testament.

With this in mind, look at the other pair of words, "Spirit" and "wind." Both come from the Hebrew word *rûwach*. However, in context it makes no sense to say that the "wind" from God "brooded" over the water. But it does make sense to say that the "Spirit" "brooded" upon the face of the water. Spirits can brood, but wind can only blow.

So why then have Jewish translators always chosen the illogical word "wind" rather than the contextually sensible word "spirit?" Because to speak of God the Creator in one breath and then God the Spirit in another is to do violence to the *Shema*. "Hear O Israel, the Lord our God, the Lord is *one*" (emphasis mine). It would appear that the plural nature of God must be avoided at any cost by Jewish translators, even if it means being illogical in word choice.

Even the Masoretic text of the Old Testament (a minute and detailed scholarly Hebrew study that took four hundred years to complete and is the accepted authority in Judaism) is closer to the Hebrew of Genesis 1:2 than the King James Bible:

> Now the earth was unformed and void, and darkness was upon the face of the deep; and the *spirit* of God *hovered* over the face of the waters (emphasis mine).

Isaiah 9:6

A more serious example of traditional bias among Jewish translators appears in Isaiah 9:6, that great Messianic prophecy pointing to Jesus. Here is how it appears in non-Jewish English Bibles:

> For unto us a child is born, unto us a son is given: and the government shall be upon his shoulder: and his name shall be called Wonderful, Counseller, The

Mighty God, The everlasting Father, The Prince of Peace."

Notice that two of the five titles ascribed to the child clearly denote deity: "The Mighty God" and "The Everlasting Father."

Now look at this same passage from the Isaac Lesser translation for Jewish readers:

> For a child is born unto us, a son hath been given unto us, and the government is placed on his shoulders; and his name is called, wonderful, counselor of the mighty God, of the everlasting Father, the Prince of peace.

Interesting, is it not, that all vestige of divinity has been stripped from the child here, and now he is simply a counselor of God. This, of course, is to be expected of Jewish translators whose traditional bias dictates that they cannot ascribe deity to any human being, not even to the virgin-born child whose very conception was brought about by the *Ruwach ha-Kodesh* (the Holy Spirit).

The traditional bias expressed in Jewish translations of Isaiah 9:6 is to be expected. However, what is not expected is to find that same bias in the "Septuagint," a translation from Hebrew to Greek which predates the birth of Jesus by 150 years. One would expect, therefore, that it would be free of any anti-Christian theology since there was no Christianity at that time. But Jewish bias *does* appear in the "Septuagint." This is how Isaiah 9:6 is rendered:

> Because for us a child is born, and to us a son is given, whose government is on his own shoulder;

> and his name is called The Messenger of Great Counsel. For I will bring peace on the rulers and health for him.

There is absolutely no mention here of the child being in any way Divine. Considering that when this was translated, the Lord Jesus would not be born for another 150 years, one cannot help but wonder why such an obvious effort was made at separating Divinity from the child. The answer seems to lie in traditional Jewish bias against any human being having Divine attributes.

One must remember that the "Septuagint" was written on the Isle of Pharos in Alexandria Harbor, Egypt, by 72 rabbinical translators who had complete rabbinical approval from the Palestine Synod. Little wonder, then, that the "Septuagint" reflects a Jewish theological slant in its translation.

Isaiah 53:5-8

A really feeble attempt by Jewish interpreters to isolate Jesus from all of the Old Testament prophecies pointing to Him is found regarding the fifty-third chapter of Isaiah:

> But *he* was wounded for *our* transgressions, *he* was bruised for *our* iniquities: the chastisement of *our* peace was put upon *him*: and with *his* stripes *we* are healed.
>
> All *we* like sheep have gone astray; *we* have turned everyone to his own way; and the LORD hath laid on *him* the iniquity of *us* all.
>
> *He* was oppressed, and *he* was afflicted, yet *he* opened not his mouth. . . .

> For *he* was cut off out of the land of the living: for the transgression of *my* people was *he* stricken (Isaiah 53:5-8, emphasis mine).

The first point to be made about this Messianic passage is that rabbinic comment on it is rare. Jewish commentators have mostly avoided writing on this passage of scripture, for obvious reasons. However, when one does come across such commentary, almost without exception the observation is made that this entire passage is a picture of Israel suffering on behalf of mankind. In his book, *Where Judaism Differed*, Abba Hillel Silver put it this way:

> The "Servant of the Lord" in Second Isaiah was the covenanted people of Israel who in the fulfillment of its divine mission would endure much suffering for the healing of the nations.[1]

This brings up the issue of "forced interpretation," for Isaiah clearly draws a distinction between "he" and "him" (the one who is doing the suffering) and "our," "we," and "us" (the ones who are the beneficiaries of that suffering). Also, Isaiah says that "for the transgression of *my* people was *he* stricken" (Isaiah 53:8, emphasis mine). Who were Isaiah's people? Why, the Jews of course. If you accept Judaism's insistence that "he" and "him" represent Jews, then what you end up with is a passage which states that the Jews are suffering as victims of the Jews. This is not only bad logic, it is bad biblical exegesis.

Isaiah 7:14

There is yet one more passage of scripture which Jewish translators have not faithfully reproduced. Isaiah 7:14 is clearly a Messianic prediction:

> Therefore the Lord himself shall give you a sign; Behold, a virgin shall conceive, and bear a son, and shall call his name Immanuel.

Two words in this passage need to be considered: "sign" and "virgin." The context of the verse is that king Ahaz was terrified at the possibility of having his power usurped. Isaiah tells him that God is surely on his side, and to prove it, Ahaz should ask of God a sign. But not any old sign—it should be a miraculous one. Ahaz is reluctant to do this, so God Himself speaks that wonderful prophecy through Isaiah.

Now among the several meanings of the word "sign" (*ôwth* in Hebrew) is "miracle," which perhaps should be used by all translators when considering the very nature of the birth being prophesied. Even Rashi, the most respected biblical and talmudic commentator not only of the Middle Ages but even of today, says that the Hebrew word, *ôwth*, in this passage, indicates a miracle and that no ordinary birth could fit the description.

With this in mind, look now at the word "virgin," which all modern Jewish translators render either "maiden" or "young woman." True, the Hebrew word here is *alma*, "maiden," and one cannot help but wonder why Isaiah did not instead use *besulah*, which in Hebrew denotes a virgin. However, the prophet avoided using *besulah* because it had also come to mean a "young married woman:"

> Lament like a virgin [*besulah*] girded with sackcloth for the husband of her youth (Joel 1:8).

Considering that this had to be a miraculous birth, Isaiah chose the word that best conveyed such an idea, *alma*, "maiden," not *besulah*, "young married woman." After all, a married woman or an immoral woman who gives birth certainly could not logically be called a "maiden." Even the "Septuagint" translation of this passage (150 years before the birth of Jesus) rendered it, "Behold, the virgin shall conceive. . . ."

Again, in an effort to put as much distance as possible between Jewish tradition and the virgin birth of Jesus Christ, Jewish translators have almost always rendered "virgin" as "maiden" or "young woman." Certainly this is far from what the prophet Isaiah had in mind, yet it is one more example of how traditional bias can pervert integrity in translation.

Even Heinrich Gesenius, grammarian and pioneer in the study of biblical Hebrew (a study incidentally free from theological considerations), said that *besulah* could be translated as "a virgin just married" or as "a young married woman." It seems quite evident, therefore, that Isaiah faithfully conveyed what God wanted him to convey, that indeed a virgin would one day give birth to Immanuel—God in our midst.

Doctrinal Biases Should Be Set Aside in Scriptural Translations

We are all admittedly biased to one degree or another, and we all show bias toward one thing or another. This appears to be an inescapable fact of human nature. However, it does not seem unreasonable to expect a translator to set aside his bias when transmitting the Word of God. Religious dogmatism has no place here.

Perhaps the English philosopher, John Stuart Mills, put it best when he said that if you have a religious doctrine, you cannot hide it under the altar, but you must put it out in plain sight where it can be examined by all. If it proves to be valid, it will persevere. However, if it proves to be false, then what you have is no longer a living spiritual truth but a dead religious dogma. My Jewish people cannot hide the obvious truth of the Messiahship of Jesus behind inaccurate Bible translations. God will not be silenced, nor will His Word be perverted.

12

Putting Words in Jesus' Mouth

A Siege Mentality: Keeping Jews from Examining Jesus' Messianic Claims

For almost two thousand years there has existed a partition of separation between Jews and Christians concerning the place of Jesus in Judaism. Even today, among some rabbis, there remains a siege mentality against Christ which they feel permits their being less than honest in their scholarship if it serves their purpose of keeping Jews from seriously considering the claims of Jesus as their Messiah.

Such a revelation appeared in a national Jewish publication in 1960. The situation came about as a consequence of an article by a Jewish writer, Norman Cousins. It was entitled, "The Jewishness of Jesus." In part, Mr. Cousins said the following:

> There is every reason for Judaism to lose its reluctance toward Jesus. His own towering spiritual presence is a projection of Judaism, not a repudiation of it. . . . He was proud to be a Jew, yet he did not confine himself to Judaism. He did not believe in spiritual exclusivity for either Jew or Gentile. He asserted

> the Jewish heritage and sought to preserve and exalt its values, but he did it within a universal context. No other figure—spiritual, philosophical, political, or intellectual—has had a greater impact on human history.[1]

Of the dozens of manuscripts that poured into *American Judaism* as a response to Mr. Cousins' article, the editors decided to publish the one written by Rabbi Roland B. Gittelsohn. It was entitled, "Not So Simple, Mr. Cousins." In this emotionally restrained but intellectually flawed essay, the rabbi points out that Norman Cousins is not talking about opening Jewish hearts to only one Jesus, he asserts that in fact there are actually three, and he asks which one Cousins is talking about.

The rabbi described the three as (1) Jesus the Jewish sage of the superfluous statement, (2) Jesus the teacher of doctrines inconsistent with Judaism, and (3) Jesus the claimed Messiah—the supposedly virgin-born, incarnate God, and fulfillment of Hebrew prophecy.

Rabbi Gittelsohn quickly eliminates the first Jesus by pointing out that much of what He taught came straight out of Judaism, and therefore presented nothing new. Jesus' teachings, he says, were in fact superfluous. Jesus' God of love, the Golden Rule, and the Beatitudes came from the Torah and were therefore familiar to all Jews. The rabbi concludes: why would Jews flock to Jesus, a mere "carbon copy of Judaism," when they already possessed the original.

In the essay the third Jesus is summarily disposed of by the rabbi's pointing out that any mortal claiming to be equal with God does particular violence to the basic tenet of Judaism. That is to say that in the Jewish perspective there is one and only one God. The rabbi points out that this Jesus who claims to be the second person of a three-member Godhead is central to Christianity—but not to Judaism.

What Did Jesus Mean?

It is with the second Jesus, the one whose teachings are supposed to be antithetical to Judaism, that Rabbi Gittelsohn is most concerned. There are four statements made by Jesus which the rabbi singles out for scrutiny:

1. that celibacy is the noblest goal of sexual expression;
2. that morality has nothing to do with politics;
3. that because some people are rich, that alone will keep them from entering heaven; and
4. that men should not resist evil but love their enemies.

Before examining these propositions, there is one question which should be foremost in your mind as a reader of this work: "What did Jesus *mean*, not what did He actually say?"

The first of Jesus' teachings that Rabbi Gittelsohn perverts is found in Matthew 19:9-12:

> And I say unto you, Whosoever shall put away his wife, except it be for fornication, and shall marry another, committeth adultery: and who so marrieth her which is put away doth commit adultery.
>
> His disciples say unto him, If the case of the man be so with his wife, it is not good to marry.
>
> But he said unto them, All men cannot receive this saying save they to whom it is given.
>
> For there are some eunuchs, which were so born from their mother's womb: and there are some eunuchs, which were made eunuchs of men: and there be eunuchs, which have made themselves eunuchs for the kingdom of heaven's sake. He that is able to receive it, let him receive it.

To Jesus' teaching about divorce, the disciples conclude that it is better to forget marriage and remain celibate than to get trapped in an unhappy marriage. Jesus then cautions them about this rush to celibacy. In essence He says that there are three kinds of eunuchs and only one of the three actually chooses to be so—he who is doing it for spiritual reasons.

Notice that twice the Lord warns His disciples that this path of voluntary celibacy is certainly not for everyone. He says: "He that is able to receive it . . ." This statement appears to mean: do not force the interpretation. Do not assume that I am talking about all men or even about most men. In point of fact, 2000 years of religious history reveals that other than for Catholic priests, very few pious men have chosen to be celibate for the kingdom of heaven's sake.

Scripture Twisting—Portraying Passages Incorrectly through Altered Meanings

Now look at what Rabbi Gittelsohn says about this teaching:

> The second Jesus . . . *recommended* celibacy, for example, as the *noblest goal* of human sexual conduct, *specifically praising* those who "make themselves eunuchs for the kingdom of heaven's sake" (emphasis mine).[2]

Aside from misinterpreting Jesus' meaning here, Rabbi Gittelsohn deliberately puts words in Jesus' mouth and erroneously argues that Jesus emphasized three things in this passage of scripture: (1) that He "recommended" celibacy; (2) that He claimed that celibacy was the "noblest goal" of sexual behavior; and (3) that He "specifically praised" those who made themselves eunuchs for God's sake.

Now unless language has no meaning, nowhere within this passage of scripture can one find such emphasis placed by Jesus as the rabbi claims. This is nothing less than a violation of literary honesty aimed at putting Jesus outside the scope of Jewish teaching. Yes, celibacy has always been abhorrent to Jews, but as we have seen, celibacy is *not* what Christ was advocating.

The second teaching of Jesus which Rabbi Gittelsohn focuses on is found in Matthew 22:17-21:

> Tell us therefore, What thinkest thou? Is it lawful to give tribute unto Caesar, or not?

But Jesus perceived their wickedness, and said, Why tempt ye me, ye hypocrites?

Show me the tribute money. And they brought unto him a penny.

And he saith unto them, Whose is this image and superscription?

They say unto him, Caesar's. Then saith he unto them, Render therefore unto Caesar the things which are Caesar's; and unto God the things that are God's.

The rabbi's comment on this passage is as follows:

> The second Jesus, in effect, taught that morality has nothing to do with politics, that the two are altogether separate categories of experience. He said, "Give unto Caesar that which is Caesar's and unto God that which is God's." Judaism insists that morality enters into every area of life, including that of politics; that nothing belongs to Caesar unless first it has been consecrated by the values we associate with God.[3]

First of all, it appears that the good rabbi overlooked the passage in John 19:15 where Pilate asks of the Jewish chief priests, "Shall I crucify your king [Jesus]? to which they answered, "We have no king but Caesar." Does Judaism "consecrate" and associate as a "value" of God, Israel's allegiance to Caesar as their one and only king? I think not.

What Jesus is teaching here is no different from what the Pharisees were teaching at the time, that the existing government (Rome) must be obeyed (which also was taught by Paul in Romans 13:1, 2). However, as Israel Abrahams, teacher of rabbinic and talmudic literature at Cambridge, pointed out:

> Though thus prepared to obey Rome and abide by all its lawful regulations, there was to be no compromise when Caesar infringed the sphere which appertained to God."[4]

For Rabbi Gittelsohn to force such an interpretation upon this teaching of Jesus is to accuse Christ of deliberately dividing the world into secular and sacred realms in which a Caesar's power is totally independent of God's sovereign authority over all mankind. If you accept the rabbi's flawed logic, then you must also agree with the Nazis who stood trial in Nuremberg and proclaimed their innocence in the Holocaust because they were simply following orders—simply rendering unto Caesar that obedience which is owed Caesar. By extension, one must also agree that conscience has no place in secular matters. The whole thing is ridiculous in the extreme.

The third teaching of Jesus, attacked by Rabbi Gittelsohn, is found in Luke 16:19-29. It is the parable of the rich man and Lazarus the beggar. The rabbi's observation concerning this passage is as follows:

> The second Jesus castigated the rich purely because they were rich. In the parable of the rich man and Lazarus, the former inherits hell not because he has committed any evil but plainly and simply because he possesses wealth.[5]

This kind of biblical exegesis is an insult to common sense. What is "plainly" and "simply" obvious here to the rabbi certainly escapes me. Nowhere in the Gospel does Jesus, or for that matter any of the writers of the New Testament, condemn wealth for its own sake. It is not money that is evil; it is the excessive *love* of money that is condemned.

For example, Rabbi Gittelsohn cites Jesus' words, "It is easier for a camel to go through the eye of a needle than for a rich man to enter the kingdom of God" (Matthew 19:24), as proof that Christ taught that wealthy people cannot enter heaven. What the rabbi conveniently omits is the context in which those words were spoken. In short, a rich young ruler offers to become a follower of Jesus. However, when Christ tells him to first sell all that he has and give it to the poor, the young man goes away in sorrow because he cannot bear to part with his wealth—not even for the kingdom of God. This occasioned Jesus' statement about how difficult it is for wealthy people to enter heaven.

Jesus is not condemning houses or barns or stocks or bonds or cars or any other symbol of affluence. He is condemning the avaricious love of those things—the greed and possessiveness that stands between man and his God. If Rabbi Gittelsohn cannot see that, then to what purpose is his much learning?

Finally, the rabbi's fourth criticism of Jesus is that He taught men not to resist evil and to love their enemies. The rabbi stated it this way:

> Whosoever smiteth thee on thy right cheek, turn to him the other also. And if any . . . would take away thy coat, let him have thy cloak also. Thus did Jesus articulate his doctrine of non-resistance to evil, another emphasis completely contradictory to

> Judaism . . . The second Jesus urged his followers to love their enemies. Judaism is far too realistic and sober a faith to endorse so psychologically impossible a precept as that.[6]

Rabbi Gittelsohn is absolutely correct when he says that passive submission to evil is repugnant to Judaism, as is the idea that one should love one's enemy. But herein lies precisely the difference between Judaism and Christianity, between Law and Grace. Christianity does not negate Judaism; it fulfills it through the atoning death of Jesus the Messiah. Grace does not negate Law but rather raises it a step closer to enabling men to live truly righteous lives that are pleasing to God.

Of course the concept of loving one's enemy is incomprehensible to Jews, who are on the outside looking in at the peace and joy and power possessed by those who have received the Spirit of God. Loving one's enemy is certainly hard enough for Christians to achieve; it is nigh impossible for those who know not Jesus and have never "internalized" their devotion toward God. In this, the good rabbi's criticism of Jesus' teaching is understandable.

A Poignant Reply

Perhaps the most poignant reply to Rabbi Gittelsohn's article came from Norman Cousins himself. In a published follow-up to the rabbi's essay, Mr. Cousins in part said the following:

> The pivotal point in your commentary has to do with your assumption that I am asking Jews to "accept" Jesus. You then go on to consider different

roles of Jesus in his relationship to Jews. If I had asked Jews to "accept" Jesus, everything you say in this part of your discussion would be valid. But my purpose in writing the article was not to persuade Jews to "accept" Jesus or Christianity or any other religion. I wanted Jews to be objective about Jesus, to free him of stigma for the persecution carried on in his name, to take pride in him as one of the two or three greatest spiritual figures in human history, and to evaluate his ideas outside of the contest of religious orthodoxy or competitions. At the very least, I wanted my fellow Jews to get over the feeling that too many of them have—a feeling of uneasiness or discomfort when the name Jesus is mentioned. In short, I wanted them, as I said in my article, to live openly with the fact of Jesus and to give full weight to the fact that He was a Jew.[7]

A Plea for Literacy, Historical and Doctrinal Honesty

So, what may be learned from all of this? It is that there is nothing surprising in uneducated people making unjustified statements based on faulty logic. But it is quite something else to find an erudite rabbi using such reasoning.

For a highly-respected leader of the Jewish community to so convolute the meaning of Jesus' teachings as to discredit Him as a Jew and make Him appear as one who has nothing of value to say to other Jews, is reprehensible. It is in fact the length to which some Jewish clerics will go to avoid the unavoidable—the Messiahship and Deity of Jesus Christ.

13

Like Lambs to the Slaughter

Where Was Their Will to Live?

That six million Jews were exterminated in Hitler's gas chambers is revolting and despicable. But it is historically true.

However, that six million Jews passively walked into those gas chambers like lambs being led to the slaughter defies all credibility. Where was their will to live? Where was their outrage against so monstrous an injustice?

These were the questions asked by *sabras* (native-born Israelis) of Holocaust survivors who came to Israel after the war. Because it was so difficult for these victims to make the young *sabras* understand the hopeless situation in which the Jews of the ghettos and then of the concentration camps found themselves, the survivors simply said nothing in their own defense. In fact, not until the 1961 trial in Israel of Adolph Eichmann (the Nazi responsible for transporting the Jews to death camps) was the Holocaust openly discussed in Israel by those who had survived it.

Jewish Uprising Against Their Tormentors

Admittedly there were Jews who *did* fight back against their German tormentors, as witnessed in the heroic defense of the Warsaw Ghetto from January to June of 1943. In fact, contrary to the widely-held concept of many Gentiles that Jews are long-suffering pacifists who lack the will to defend themselves, history proves otherwise. The Old Testament is replete with examples of Hebrews defending themselves against Gentile aggressors.

Of special historical note is the Maccabean revolt (168-167 B.C.) against the Syrian, Antiochus Epiphanes, who ordered that sacrifices to Greek deities be offered on Jewish altars in every city and village in Judea.

Another particularly defiant act of Jewish resistance to Gentile aggression occurred at Masada, where 960 Jews held off Roman legions for three years (70-73 A.D.), ending only when the Jews chose suicide rather than surrender.

Then, too, there was the Bar Kokhba Revolt of 132-135 A.D. against the tyranny of Rome. So fierce was the fighting that Rome's ablest general, Julius Severus, was brought all the way from Britain to Judea to take charge of what had become a full-blown war. After three years of fighting and starvation, the cost to the Jews of this rebellion was 985 villages destroyed and 580,000 Jews killed.

Passive Acceptance of Gentile Pogroms

Yet, despite proven Jewish determination not to submit to injustice and persecution, beginning in the Middle Ages Jews in Europe (particularly in Russia) began passively accepting the dreaded Gentile pogroms with their periodic pillaging, beatings, and even murders of innocent Jews. In fact, Jewish mothers traditionally taught their children that "If a goy [Gentile] hits you, bow your head and he will spare your life."

This passive acceptance of Gentile persecution eventually became the norm for Jews throughout much of Europe for the next five hundred years—certainly well into the twentieth century. As one Jewish writer observed:

> This right to lynch was a kind of unwritten law which nobody dreamed of contesting—a fact that was accepted, admitted, and taught from generation to generation in both communities [i.e. in Jewish and Gentile].[1]

But beyond this historic Jewish acceptance of Gentile persecution, the most revealing issue for Christians regarding the Holocaust is not the fact that Jews passively walked into Nazi gas chambers but rather the attitude those Jews held toward their own impending doom. These attitudes were of two kinds: secular and religious.

Jean-Francois Steiner was only two years old when his family died in concentration camps. After the war, he had a compelling desire to know why the Jews went to their deaths, apparently without resistance. The results of his search for answers provided not only the background for his soul-wrenching book, *Treblinka*, but also revealed some of the attitudes held by ghetto Jews toward their imminent deaths.

Treblinka was one of six Nazi killing centers. In August, 1943, six hundred armed inmates of the more than 800,000 who ultimately died there revolted, attacked the guards, burned the camp, and fled into the forest. Of these six hundred, only 40 survived. Steiner personally interviewed as many of these 40 as were willing to recount their past horror to him.

Of the many insights gained by Steiner from these survivors, one fact in particular relates directly to the question of Jewish submission to the Nazis. On rare occasions someone would escape from one of the camps and return to the ghetto (there being nowhere else to go) with the news that those being deported from the ghettos were not being taken to work camps but were being put to death.

Four Attitudes Concerning Jewish Deaths

One of the attitudes held by some Jews in the ghetto toward this news was total disbelief. It simply defied reason and logic that the Germans would kill all of the Jews. Why? For what possible purpose? It made absolutely no sense to kill tens of thousands of workers who could otherwise be useful to the German war effort. No, they reasoned, these reports of the mass killing of Jews had to be the result of hysteria and exaggeration.

There was also another attitude held by many of the ghetto Jews. They believed that if they didn't resist, if they passively submitted to German authority, the Nazis would not really go through with the killings. After all, had not the Jews of countless generations submitted to the pogroms and yet survived—beaten and bruised, certainly—but alive? The age-old Jewish mentality was still operating here: "If a goy hits you, bow your head and he will spare your life." So tens of thousands of Jews must have passively walked into the gas chambers believing that the Germans would not ultimately carry out their intentions—not really. "Remember, just keep your head bowed and your life will be spared."

A third attitude was held by some pious Hebrews who believed that the killing of Jews on so massive a scale must be a Divine warning to the world at large. Others held that the killings were God's warning only to Jews themselves. In either case, those who understood their impending deaths as part of an unknown but nevertheless Divine plan rather than as some arbitrary, capricious action of man over which God had no control, believed that they dare not resist. If this was the will of God, so be it.

Finally, there was a fourth attitude held by some Jews regarding the reports of the mass killings taking place in the camps. This view is best expressed in Abraham Ezra Millgram's book, *Great Jewish Ideas*:

> They [those Jews facing Hitler's gas chambers] really believed that their suffering and all of the evil that was then ruling the world, were the *Hevely Mashia* "the birth-pangs of the Messiah." For it is established Jewish doctrine, that even as a woman

> who is about to give birth and thus to perform the most marvelous act of human creation must first undergo great pain, so also the world will be torn by terrible wars . . . immediately before the Kingdom of God will be established on earth by the Messiah.
>
> They [the Jews of Europe] truly thought that through their own convulsions they were helping to give birth to a radically new and better world under the immediate sovereignty of God, and they firmly expected the person of the Messiah to appear shortly to usher in this new age.[2]

Heartbreaking? Yes, but these pious Jews who believed that it required their own deaths to bring about the Kingdom of God on earth were more than willing to be sacrificed. This example of their faith was touchingly recorded by the son of Rabbi Israel Shapira of Gradsiks:

> When the people of the camp, by the thousands, were brought into the forecourt of the chambers of destruction in Treblinka, they turned to the rabbi and said: "Our rabbi, what do you say now?" The holy rabbi answered them quietly: "Hearken, my brothers and my sisters, O people of God! We may not criticize God's deeds. If it has been determined that in this time, at this stage of the process of redemption, we are to be sacrifices of the agonies of the Messiah, that we are to go on the stake, happy are we that we have been given such meritorious opportunity. . . . I command you not to panic and not to weep as you go into the oven but rather to be joyous, with the song *Ani Ma'amin* [faith in the coming of the Messiah], and like Rabbi Akiba to die with the word 'one' of the *Shema* on your lips." The people obeyed the words of the holy one, and singing *Ani Ma'amin* and reciting the *Shema Yisrael* they publicly sanctified God. May God keep them, and may their memory be blessed.[3]

Negative Observations on the Nature of Man

No one will ever know what was really in the heart of each and every Jew as he or she walked into those gas chambers. But we can conclude several truths concerning the four attitudes they held.

First, those Jews who refused to believe that one human being could do to another what the Nazis were doing to the Jews reveals the utter depth of depravity to which the heart of man can sink. Certainly this is more in keeping with the perception some Christians hold of man as being utterly depraved than it is in supporting the Jewish view of man as being basically moral and good.

Secondly, the hopeless resignation with which some Jews accepted their fate, simply because they had always been brutalized by non-Jews, also reveals the evil propensity of the human heart to exploit and debase one's fellow man. God Himself summed it up when He said, "for the imagination of man's heart is evil from his youth; . . ." (Genesis 8:21).

Positive Observations on the Nature of Man

But there also are positive aspects reflected in the attitudes of some Jews who foresaw their own deaths in the Holocaust.

First, those who saw their imminent destruction as being either a Divine warning to mankind in general, or to Jews in particular, reflected the submission of all pious people to the will of God, even if that will and purpose works to their own demise. In this, one can hear the words of Job: "Though he slay me, yet will I trust him" (Job 13:15). And what is the nature of that spiritual trust? It is blind, unquestioned obedience, no matter what!

The other positive reflection seen in Jewish attitudes regarding the injustice of their own imminent deaths was that they were making a better world possible—a Messianic rule of universal love and peace and justice among all men everywhere. Such thinking has to represent the pinnacle of spiritual selflessness, be it Jewish or Christian.

Did Jews passively walk into Hitler's gas chambers? By and large, yes, but only because in so doing, many of them believed that they were either yielding to God's will or that they were helping to usher in the coming of the Messiah. Both of these reasons are understandable to Christians, but incomprehensible to those who have no personal relationship with God.

Certainly no rational person harbors a death wish, for life is too precious. Yet, those whose lives are bound up and intertwined with God's see forfeiture of life as no great loss. As Paul the apostle put it: "For to me to live is Christ, and to die is gain" (Philippians 1:21).

Conclusion

What, then, has been revealed in this brief study? What understanding do we as Christians now have concerning God's ancient people?

The Need for Internalized Worship

Perhaps the most important realization is also the most heartbreaking, that for thousands of years God has always been "out there" somewhere for the Jew, but perhaps not in his heart. Either God was in the burning bush or on the heights of Sinai or in the pillar of cloud by day or in the pillar of fire by night or in the Holy of Holies in the tabernacle or in the temple, but always He was "out there," always outside the heart of Israel.

The real problem is that most Jews have never been able to "internalize" God because of their perception of Him. For example, even the most pious Jews could never bring themselves to call the LORD GOD, "Father," as do Christians. This is because of the Jews' profound reverence toward God's unspeakable Holiness. In fact, orthodox Jews never fully write out God's name but reduce to to a Hebrew tetragrammaton (transliterated YHWH—JeHoVaH—or YAHWEH). Even among present-day Jewish writers, many never write "God" but instead render it "G-D."

Judaism has always believed that diligent observance of ritual and tradition would please Jehovah. Yet that is not what God Himself would have them do. Listen to Isaiah:

> To what purpose is the multitude of your sacrifices unto me? saith the Lord: I am full of the burnt offerings of rams, and the fat of fed beasts; and I delight not in the blood of bullocks, or of lambs, or of he goats . . .
>
> Bring no more vain oblations; incense is an abomination unto me;
>
> Your new moons and your appointed feasts my soul hateth: they are a trouble unto me; I am weary of bearing them (Isaiah 1:11, 13, 14).

What, then, is left for Jews if they cannot reach out to God through ritual and traditional observance? Paul the apostle clearly saw their problem and defined it:

> For he is not a Jew, which is one outwardly; neither is that circumcision which is outward in the flesh:
>
> But he is a Jew, which is one inwardly; and circumcision is that of the heart, in the spirit, and not in the letter; whose praise is not of men, but of God (Romans 2:28, 29).

This need for Jews to internalize their worship of God was declared by the Lord Himself through the prophet Jeremiah:

> Behold, the days come, saith the Lord, that I will make a new covenant with the house of Israel, and with the house of Judah:
>
> But this shall be the covenant that I will make with the house of Israel: After those days, saith the LORD, I will put my law in their inward parts, and write it in

> their hearts; and will be their God, and they shall be my people (Jeremiah 31:31, 33).

For the Jew, the altar of sacrifice is gone, along with the temple. Today Judaism is fractured and fragmented into denominations. Beyond this, many Jews no longer even have time for the God of Israel.

Pray That the Jews May Recognize Their Messiah

What, then, should be our feeling toward the Jewish people in their quest to lay hold of their God who has always remained somehow aloof and unattainable?

Perhaps we might take our cue from the most revered Jew in Christendom (aside from the Lord Jesus), the apostle Paul, who, baring his heart to us, wrote:

> . . . I have great heaviness and continual sorrow in my heart.
>
> For I could wish that I myself were accursed from Christ for my brethren, my kinsmen according to the flesh (Romans 9:2, 3).

Also,

> Brethren, my heart's desire and my prayer to God for Israel [the Jews] is, that they may be saved.
>
> For I bear record that they have a zeal of God, but not according to knowledge (Romans 10:1, 2).

Pray, will you, that the scales might fall from the eyes of God's ancient people, that they may at last recognize their long-awaited Messiah, Jesus.

May the God of Abraham, Isaac, and Jacob bless and keep you until He who loved us and washed us from our sins in His own blood returns for those whose eyes are toward heaven, looking for that "blessed hope."

Endnotes

1. The Jew: Both an Enigma and an Anomaly

1 Ernst van den Haag, *The Jewish Mystique* (New York: Stein and Day, 1969), p. 22.
2 *Ibid.*, pp. 22-23.
3 *Ibid.*, p. 23.
4 *Ibid.*
5 *Ibid.*

2. How Does One Define a Jew?

1 Lawrence H. Scheffman, *Who Was A Jew?* (Hobo ken: KTAV Publishing House, 1985), p. 61.

3. A Diminished Spiritual Vitality?

1 Max Brod, *The Dawn* (Pittsburgh: 1934), p. 24. No publisher given.
2 Heschel, Speech given at the Fifty-third Annual Convention of Conservative Rabbis in Atlanta City, 1955.
3 *Ibid.*
4 Joseph Zeitlin *Disciples of the Wise* (Chicago: Quadrangle Books, 1974), pp. 142-145.
5 Joel Blau, *The Jewish Spectator*, January, 1949, p. 17.
6 Nathan A. Barack, *The Contemporary Jewish Record*, Aug., 1942, p. 13.
7 *The Jewish Spectator*, April, 1949, p. 24.
8 Nathan Glazer, *Commentary*, Vol. 6, No. 2, 1956, p. 12.
9 "Bringing Jews to Jesus in Russia" by Rachel Katz, *Moment* Vol. 22 No. 1, February, 1997, p. 48.
10 *Ibid.*, p. 49.
11 *Ibid.*, p. 50.

4. THE DIVISIONS OF JUDAISM

1 "So They Say We're Not Jews," *The Jewish Journal* Vol. 12 No. 5, March 28-April 3, 1997, p. 4.
2 Joseph L. Blau, *Modern Varieties of Judaism* (New York: Columbia U. Press, 1966), p. 105.
3 Marc Lee Raphael, *Profiles in American Judaism* (San Francisco: Harper & Row, 1988), p. 15.
4 Joseph L. Blau, *Modern Varieties of Judaism* (New York: Columbia University Press, 1966), p. 176.

5. CHRISTIANITY AND ANTI-SEMITISM

1 Leo Trepp, *Eternal Faith Eternal People* (New York: Prentice-Hall, 1962), p. 390.
2 *Ibid.*, p. 391.
3 Robert S. Wistrich, *Anti-Semitism The longest Hatred* (New York: Pantheon Books, 1991), p. 25.
4 Charles Y. Glock and Rodney Stark, *Christian Beliefs and Anti-Semitism* (New York: Harper & Row, 1996), p. 148.
5 Geoffrey Wigder ed., *Encyclopedia of Judaism* (New York: 1989), p. 166.
6 Glock and Stark, p. 160.
7 *Ibid.*, p. 149.
8 Wigder, *op. cit.*, p. 166.
9 Wistrich, *op. cit.*, p. 28.
10 Glock and Stark, *op. cit.*, p. 148.
11 *Ibid.*, p. 148.
12 Leon Poliakiv, *The History of Anti-Semitism* (New York: The Vanguard Press, 1973), pp. 183-184.

6. WHY JEWS DON'T ACCEPT JESUS AS THE SON OF GOD

1 David Cooper, *Israel's God* (Los Angeles: Biblical Research Institute, 1953), p. 37.
2 *The Torah A Modern Commentary* (New York: Union of American Hebrew Congregations, 1981), p. 24.

7. WHY JEWS REJECTED JESUS AS THEIR MESSIAH

1 Abraham Ezra Millgram, *Great Jewish Ideas* (Clinton, Mass: B'nai B'rith, Colonial Press, 1964), p. 247.

8. A JEWISH PARADOX

1 "What Life Means To Einstein" by George S. Viereck, *Saturday Evening Post*, October 26, 1929.
2 Leo Trepp, *Eternal Faith Eternal People* (New York: Prentice-Hall, 1962), p. 147.
3 Elliot N. Dorff, *Conservative Judaism: Our Ancestors To Our Descendants* (New York: United Synagogues of America, 1978), p. 236.
4 Trepp, *op. cit.*, p. 147.
5 Dorff, *op. cit.*, p. 236.
6 Trepp, *op. cit.*, p. 147.
7 Dorff, *op. cit.*, p. 236.
8 David Cooper, *Israel's Messiah* (Los Angeles: Biblical Research Institute, 1955), p. 92.

9. JEWISH ATTITUDES TOWARD SIN

1 Abba Hillel Silver, *Where Judaism Differed* (Philadelphia: Jewish Publication Society, 1956), p. 171.
2 C.G. Montefiore and H. Loewe, *A Rabbinic Anthology* (Philadelphia: Jewish Publication Society, 1960), pp. 295-296.
3 *Ibid.*, p. 296.
4 *Ibid.*, p. 301.
5 *Ibid.*, p. 302.

10. TWO DATES THAT CHANGED JUDAISM FOREVER

1 Ernest R. Trattner, *Understanding The Talmud* (New York: Thomas Nelson & Sons, 1955), p. 36.
2 Nahum N. Glatzer, *Essays In Jewish Thought* (Montgomery, AL: U. of Alabama Press, 1978), p. 49, 50.

11. BIAS IN JEWISH BIBLE TRANSLATIONS

1 Abba Hillel Silver, *Where Judaism Differed* (Philadelphia: Jewish Publication Society, 1956), p. 173.

12. PUTTING WORDS IN JESUS' MOUTH

1 "The Jewishness of Jesus" by Norman Cousins, *American Judaism* Vol. 10 No. 1, 1960, p. 8.
2 Paul Kresh ed., *American Judaism Reader* (New York Abelard-Schuman, 1967), p. 3O.
3 *Ibid.*
4 Nolan B. Harmon ed., *The Interpreter's Bible* Vol 7 (New York: Abingdon Press, 1953), p. 518.
5 Kresh, *op. cit.*, p. 31.
6 *Ibid.*
7 *Ibid.*, p. 34.

13. LIKE LAMBS TO THE SLAUGHTER

1 Jean-Francois Steiner, *Treblinka* (New York: New American Library, 1967), p. 16.
2 Abraham Ezra Millgram, *Great Jewish Ideas* (Clinton, Mass: B'hai B'rith, Colonial Press, 1964), p. 238.
3 *Ibid.*, pp. 238-239.

Selected Bibliography

NOTE: *Those sources whose publication dates make them no longer available through book sellers or not easily located in local libraries, may be found in college and university libraries.*

A Symposium Compiled by the Editor of "Commentary" Magazine. *The Condition of Jewish Belief*, New York: The Macmillian Co., 1966.

Bamberger, Bernard J. *The Search for Jewish Theology.* New York: Behrman House, Inc., 1978.

Blau, Joseph L. *Modern Varieties of Judaism.* New York: Columbia University Press, 1966.

Cohen, Arthur A. *Arguments and Doctrines (Jewish Thinking in the Aftermath of the Holocaust).* New York: Harper & Row, Publishers, 1970.

Cohen, Mark R. *Under Crescent and Cross (Jews in the Middle Ages).* Princeton, New Jersey: Princeton University Press, 1994.

Daube, David. *The New Testament and Rabbinic Judaism.* New York: Arno Press, 1973.

Eisendrath, Maurice N. *Can Faith Survive?* New York: McGraw-Hill Book Co., 1964.

Feldman, Louis H. *Jew and Gentile in the Ancient World.* Princeton, New Jersey: Princeton University Press, 1993.

Glatzer, Nahum N. *Essays in Jewish Thought.* University, Alabama: University of Alabama Press, 1978.

Guignebert, Charles. *The Jewish World in the Time of Jesus*. New Hyde Park, New York:University Books, 1965.

Harshbarger, Luther H., and John A. Mourant. *Judaism and Christianity*. Boston: Allyn and Bacon, Inc., 1968.

Heschel, Abraham Joshua. *Israel: An Echo of Eternity*. New York: Farrar, Straus, and Giroux, 1971.

Jacobs, Louis, *The Talmudic Argument*. New York: Cambridge University Press, 1984.

Katz, Steven T. *Interpreters of Judaism in the Late Twentieth Century*. Washington D.C.: B'nai b'rith Books, 1993.

Klausner, Joseph, *The Messianic Idea in Israel*. London: George Allen and Unwin Ltd., 1956.

Klein, Charlotte. *Anti-Judaism in Christian Theology*. Philadelphia: Fortress Press, 1978.

Liebes, Yehuda. *Studies in Jewish Myth and Jewish Messianism*. Albany, New York: State University of New York Press, 1993.

Liebman, Charles S., and Steven M. Cohen. *Two Worlds of Judaism*. New Haven, Connecticut: Yale University Press, 1990.

Martin, Bernard, ed., *Contemporary Reform Jewish Thought*. Chicago: Quadrangle Books, 1968.

Mussner, Franz, *Tractate On the Jews*. Philadelphia: Fortress Press, 1984.

Neusner, Jacob. *Judaism*. Chicago: University of Chicago Press, 1981.

Oberman, Heiko A. *The Roots of Anti-Semitism*. Philadelphia: Fortress Press, 1984.

Riemer, Jack, ed., *Jewish Reflections On Death*. New York: Schocken Books, 1975.

Rosen, Ruth, ed., *Jewish Doctors Meet the Great Physician.* San Francisco: Purple Pomegranate Productions, 1997.

Saperstein, Marc, ed., *Essential Papers On Messianic Movements and Personalities in Jewish History*. New York: New York University Press, 1992.

Schector, Solomon. *Aspects of Rabbinic Theology*. New York: Schocken Books, 1969.

Scholem, Gershom. *The Messianic Idea in Judaism*. New York: Schocken Books, 1971.

Scult, Mel. *Judaism Faces the Twentieth Century*. Detroit: Wayne State University Press, 1991.

Seltzer, Robert M. *Jewish People, Jewish Thought*. New York: Macmillian Publishers Inc., 1980.

Sohn, Seock-Tae. *The Divine Election of Israel*. Grand Rapids, Michigan: William B. Eerdmans Publishing Company, 1991.

Walker, Thomas T. *The Jewish People (Jewish Views of Jesus)* New York: Arno Press, 1973.

Index

—A—

Abrahams, Israel, 111
Ambros, 50
Amile, 28
anti-Semitism, 46, 48, 50
Aquinas, Thomas, 48, 50
Aronson, David, 42
atonement:
  blood, 90
  substitute, 90
Augustine, 48, 50, 53

—B—

Bar Kokhba, 116
Barack, Nathan A., 33
Ben Joachi, Simion, 58
Blau, Joel, 31
Brod, Max, 28, 29
Bouillon, Godfrey, 52
Brotkin, Ariveh, 35

—C—

Christ, 11, 14, 32, 46, 49, 50, 54, 67, 79, 82, 109, 112, 114, 122
Chrysostom, John, 49, 50
Claudel, 28

commandments, 37
Council of Trent, 76
Cousins, Norman, 105, 106, 113
Cyril, 50

—D—

Dante, 50
Day of Atonement, 81
Dostoyevsky, 29

—E—

echod, 59
Edict of Expulsion, 53
Ehrlich, Paul 16
Eichmann, Adolph, 115
Einstein, Albert, 17, 22, 67
Elohim, 57
Epiphanes, Antiochus, 116

—F—

Falasha, 21
Flannery, Edward, 50
Frankel, Zacharias, 41
Freud, Sigmund 17
Funk, Casimir, 16

—G—

Gamaliel, 63
Gemara, 88, 89
Gesenius, Heinrich, 103
ghetto, 40
Gittelsohn, Roland B., 106, 107, 109, 110, 112, 113
Glazer, Nathan, 34
Gregory VII, 50

—H—

Halakah, 20, 24, 25, 41, 88, 89
Hebrew words, 23, 29, 39, 55, 59, 60, 78, 91, 97, 99, 102, 115, 117, 119, 120
Henry II, 50
Henry VI, 50
Heschel, Abraham J., 29
Hitler, Adolph, 49, 50
Holocaust, 23, 47, 115, 117

—I—

Issi, 80

—J—

Jew:
- anomaly, 16
- conservative, 23
- contributions, 16
- definition of, 19
- enigma, 15
- orthodox, 23
- reform, 23
- smarter than, 17

Jesus, 12, 13, 14, 36, 46, 54, 60, 61, 63, 70, 74, 76, 82, 105, 106, 107, 108, 112, 113
Jewish Theological Seminary, 41
Judaism:
- Articles of Faith, 69, 72,
- conservatism, 37, 41, 56
- Declaration of Principles, 69, 72
- malnutrition, spiritual, 35
- orthodoxy, 37, 38, 42, 56
- Paradox, 67
- reconstructionism, 37, 42
- reform, 21, 37, 39, 40s

—K—

Kaplan, Mordecai, 42
Kertzer, Morris N., 40
Kirkegaard, 28
Kohut, Alexander, 41

—L—

Landsteiner, Karl, 17
Lateran Council IV, 49
Law of Return, 20
Luther, Martin, 51

—M—

Maimonides, Moses, 69, 72
Marvel, Andrew, 55
Marx, Karl, 17
Masoretic text, 98
Mendelssohm, Moses, 40
Messiah, 14, 25, 35, 41, 46, 61, 63, 64, 71, 75, 102, 120, 125
Millgram, Abraham Ezra, 66, 120
Mills, John Stuart, 104
Minofsky, 16
Mishnah, 75, 87
Moses, 30, 68, 69, 76, 87

—N—

Nazi, 22, 47, 49, 50, 51, 53, 118, 119
Nebuchadnezzar, 85
Nicodemus, 46
Nobel Prize, 16
Novalis, 28
Nuremberg, 22

—O—

Oral Law, 20, 85, 86, 87, 88

—P—

Paul the apostle, 32, 35, 76, 122, 124, 125
Pentateuch, 23, 30, 85, 86
Pope Eugenius IV, 50
Pope Innocent III, 48, 50
Population, Jewish, 16

—R—

Rashi, 102
Reichstein, Tadeus, 17
Rolvaag, O.E, 95
Rosenzweig, Franz, 59
Russian Academy of Science, 35

—S—

Salk, Jonas, 16
Sanhedrin, 62, 87
Scheffman, Lawrence H., 24
servitus judaeorum, 49
Severus, Julius, 116
Shapira, Israel, 120
Shayervich, Adolph, 35
Shema, 60, 120
Silver, Abba, 72, 76, 101
sin:
  Adam's, 76
  inclination to, 78
  inherited, 77
  original, 76
  repentance for, 79

Sinai, 32, 37
Spanish Inquisition, 53
St. Francis, 51
Steiner, Jean-François, 117
Synod of Clermont, 52
Synod of Orleans, 52
Synod of Vienna, 52

—T—

Talmud, 20, 43, 68, 88, 89
tempereta severitas, 53
Temple, 85, 90, 91, 92, 124
Third Lateran Council, 48
Titus, 85
translation, Bible:
  intentional error, 97
  King James, 95
  Septuagint, 95, 99, 100, 103
  Tyndale's, 95
  unintentional error, 96
  Vulgate, 95
  Wycliffe's, 95
Treblinka, 117
Trepp, Leo, 45

—U—

Union of Orthodox Rabbis, 39
University of Michigan, Judaic Studies, 35

—V—

van den Haag, Ernst, 17

—W—

Waksman, Selman, 17
Wise, Isaac Meyer, 42, 77

—Y—

Yâchîyd, 60
yetzer Ha-ra, 78, 79
Y'shua ha-Mashiah, 13

—Z—

Zeitlin, Joseph, 30
zionism, 34

About the Author

Marshall D. Isaacson was born and raised in a religious Jewish home in Chicago. He was taught all the traditions and conventions of his faith. He says, however, that the promises inherent in Judaism were not passed on to him. It wasn't until he and his family moved to California that he became aware of Jesus and his significance to Jews.

At the early age of 14, Marshall recognized the fact that Jesus Christ was Judaism's long-awaited Messiah. He was estranged from his family after his conversion to Christianity and had to leave home at the age of 16. Seven years passed before he saw his parents again.

In 1942, Marshall dropped out of school and joined the Merchant Marines where he served for the duration of World War II. After the War, he spent several years prospecting for gold and diving for pearls at Thursday Island, Australia. Later he became a truck driver for an aircraft company in California at night and built a 30-foot sailboat by day.

In 1962, Marshall, then married and with two small children, returned to school to finish his education. Completing high school at age 36 was a particularly challenging struggle. However, he continued on to earn bachelors and masters degrees in English, and started a doctoral program. He eventually became an assistant professor of English at a state college, and then moved to Utah where he taught at Weber State University for over 20 years until retirement.

Marshall and his wife, Joyce, now live in Ogden, Utah. They enjoy aerobic walking, bicycling, researching and writing.